T0046652

How to Talk to Anyone, Anytime, Anywhere

Other Books by Larry King

On the Line: The New Road to the White House
with Mark Stencel

*When You're from Brooklyn, Everything Else
Is Tokyo* with Marty Appel

Larry King
with Emily Yoffe

Tell It to the King
with Peter Occhiogrosso

Mr. King, You're Having a Heart Attack
with B. D. Colen

Tell Me More
with Peter Occhiogrosso

How to Talk to Anyone, Anytime, Anywhere

The Secrets of Good Communication

Larry King

WITH BILL GILBERT

 THREE RIVERS PRESS • NEW YORK

"Remember?" by Irving Berlin © 1925 by Irving Berlin.
© Copyright renewed. International copyright secured.
Used by permission. All rights reserved.

Copyright © 1994 by Larry King

All rights reserved. No part of this book may be reproduced or
transmitted in any form or by any means, electronic or mechanical,
including photocopying, recording, or by any information storage and
retrieval system, without permission in writing from the publisher.

Published by Three Rivers Press, New York, New York.
Member of the Crown Publishing Group.

Random House, Inc. New York, Toronto, London, Sydney, Auckland
www.randomhouse.com

THREE RIVERS PRESS is a registered trademark and the Three Rivers
Press colophon is a trademark of Random House, Inc.

Originally published in hardcover by Crown Publishers,
November 1994. First paperback edition printed in 1995.

Printed in the United States of America

Design by June Bennett-Tantillo

Library of Congress Cataloging-in-Publication Data
King, Larry.
How to talk to anyone, anytime, anywhere: the secrets of good
communication/Larry King with Bill Gilbert.
1. Conversation.   I. Gilbert, Bill, 1931– .   II. Title.
BJ212.K47 1994   94-31458
302.3'46—dc20   CIP
ISBN 0-517-88453-4

37th Printing

To the honored memory of Bob Woolf,
my agent and my friend.

L. K.

The Rest of Our Team

No book ever gets published by the authors alone. We did the interviewing and the writing, but others performed equally essential roles. For that we extend our gratitude, especially to:

Peter Ginna, our editor at Crown Publishers in New York.

Judy Thomas, Larry's personal assistant and his associate producer on CNN's *Larry King Live.*

Maggie Simpson, public relations director for *Larry King Live.*

Pat Piper, producer of *The Larry King Show* on the Mutual Broadcasting System for so many years.

Stacey Woolf, Larry's agent, who made this book possible in the first place.

Russell Galen, Bill's agent for many years and many books.

Contents

How to Talk to Anyone, Anytime, Anywhere

Introduction: We've All Gotta Talk

Would you rather

1. jump out of an airplane without a parachute

or

2. sit next to someone you've never met before at a dinner party?

If your answer is 1, don't feel bad. You've got a lot of company. Even though talking is something we do every day, there are lots of situations where it can be difficult and situations where we could do it better. The road to success, whether it's social or professional, is paved with talk. If you're not confident as a talker, the road can be bumpy.

That's why I've written this book—to make it

smoother. I've been talking for a living for thirty-seven years, and on my radio and TV shows I've had conversations with people from Mikhail Gorbachev to Michael Jordan. I also regularly give speeches to groups that range from sheriffs to storm-door salesmen. In the following pages I'll tell you what I have learned about how to talk, whether you're speaking to one person or a hundred.

To me, talk is one of the great pleasures of life, something I've always loved to do. One of my first memories of growing up in Brooklyn is standing on the corner of Eighty-sixth Street and Bay Parkway and announcing the makes of cars driving by. I was seven years old. My pals called me "the Mouthpiece." I've been talking ever since.

My best friend from those years, Herb Cohen (who is still my best friend), tells people about how I used to root for the Dodgers at Ebbets Field. I'd sit in the bleachers by myself, roll up my scorecard, and "broadcast" the game. Then I'd come home and tell my pals everything— and I do mean *everything*—about the game. Herb still tells people, "If Larry went to a game at Ebbets Field and the game lasted two hours and ten minutes, so did Larry's description of it." It figures that Herbie and I met each other for the first time in the principal's office when we were ten. I walked in and there he was. Today we can't really remember why we were sent there—but talking in class would be a good bet for both of us.

But as much as I enjoy talking, I know why people can be uncomfortable with it. There's the fear of saying the wrong thing, or saying the right thing in the wrong way. As one writer put it, "It is better to remain silent and be presumed a fool than to open your mouth and remove all doubt." When you're talking to a stranger, or to a lot of other people at once, the fear is magnified.

I hope this book will help take away that fear. One thing I've learned is that there's nobody you can't talk to, if you have the right attitude. After reading this book, you should be able to approach any conversation with confidence, and you'll know how to get your message across effectively in a professional setting. You'll be talking better and enjoying it more.

The chapters here cover the waterfront, with tips and real-life examples that cover talking in a variety of situations, from your cousin's wedding to a black-tie dinner party to a speech to the PTA. I'll tell you what you can learn from the guests I have talked to on the air and how you can use my own lessons—you'll see that some of them came the hard way—to help you.

Talk is the most essential form of human communication, the one that distinguishes us as a species. In fact, it's been estimated the average person speaks eighteen thousand words a day, and I don't doubt that figure at all. (It's probably more in my case.) So why not develop our skills to become the best talkers we can be? Let's start right now. Just turn the page.

Hey, Herbie, listen up!

Larry King

1

Talk 101

THE BASICS OF SUCCESSFUL CONVERSATION
- Honesty
- The right attitude
- Interest in the other person
- Openness about yourself

Talking is like playing golf, driving a car, or owning a store—the more you do it, the better you get at it, and the more fun you have doing it. But you have to understand the fundamentals first.

I've been fortunate to have achieved a certain level of success in talking. Maybe enough so that as you are reading this book, you're thinking to yourself, Oh, sure—*he* can say talking is fun. He's good at it.

It's true that talking has come naturally to me, but even those who have a natural ability for something have to work to develop it. That's what turns a talent into a skill. Ted Williams, the greatest baseball hitter I ever saw and a man blessed with more natural ability than anyone in my lifetime, took batting practice like everyone else. Luciano Pavarotti was born with a wonderful voice, but he still took singing lessons.

I have a natural ability, and inclination, to talk. But I've had plenty of moments when talk didn't come easy.

MY INAUSPICIOUS DEBUT

If you could have been a fly on the wall in a Miami Beach radio studio thirty-seven years ago and witnessed my first morning in broadcasting, you would have bet the ranch that I was the *last* guy who could even survive, much less succeed, as a professional talker.

It happened at station WAHR, a small station across the street from the police station, on First Street, just off Washington, on the morning of May 1, 1957. I had been there three weeks, hanging around, hoping to break into my dream world of radio. The station's general manager, Marshall Simmonds, told me he liked my voice (another thing I can't take any credit for), but he didn't have any openings. That didn't discourage me. I was willing to take my chances, and I told him so. He said fine—if I hung around, I'd get the job the next time he had an opening.

I had just set out from Brooklyn, knowing I could live with my uncle Jack and his wife in a small apartment within walking distance of the station while waiting for my big break. I didn't have any money, just my uncle's roof over my head for shelter. I went to the station every day, watching the disc jockeys on the air, the newscasters reporting the news, and the sportscaster giving the sports results.

I watched in silent fascination as I saw stories come over the AP and UPI wires for the first time. I wrote a few little stories myself, hoping somebody would use them on the air. Suddenly, after three weeks, the morning dee-jay quit. Marshall called me into his office on a Friday and told me I had the job, starting at nine o'clock Monday morning. I'd make fifty-five dollars a week. I'd be on from nine until noon Monday through Friday. In the afternoon I would be doing newscasts and sportscasts until getting off at five o'clock.

My dream had come true! Not only was I getting on the radio—I was going to be on for three hours at a time every morning, plus another half-dozen times or so every afternoon. I was going to be on the air as often as Arthur Godfrey, the superstar on CBS.

I didn't sleep that whole weekend. I kept rehearsing things to say on the air. By eight-thirty on my first morning, I was a basket case. I was drinking coffee and water for the dryness in my mouth and throat. I had the record with my theme song, Les Elgart's "Swingin' Down the Lane," with me, ready to cue it up on the turntable as soon as I went into the studio. In the meantime I was getting more nervous by the minute.

Then Marshall Simmonds called me into his office to wish me good luck. After I thanked him he asked, "What name are you going to use?"

I said, "What are you talking about?"

"Well, you can't use Larry Zeiger. It's ethnic. People won't be able to spell it or remember it. You need a better name. You're not going to use Larry Zeiger."

He had the *Miami Herald* open on his desk. There was a full-page ad for King's Wholesale Liquors. Marshall looked down and said simply, "How about Larry *King?*"

"Okay."

"Fine. That will be your name—Larry King. You'll host *The Larry King Show.*"

So there I was, with a new job, a new show, a new theme song, even a new name. The news comes on at nine, and I'm sitting in the studio with "Swingin' Down the Lane" cued up, ready to broadcast *The Larry King Show* to a waiting world. My mouth feels like cotton.

As my own engineer (always the case at a small station), I started the theme. The music comes on. Then I fade the music down so I can begin to talk. Only nothing comes out.

So I bring the music up again and fade it again. Still

no words coming out of my mouth. It happens a third time. The only thing my listeners are hearing is a record going up and down in volume, unaccompanied by any human voice.

I can still remember saying to myself that I'd been wrong, that I was a street gabber but I wasn't ready to do this professionally. I knew I would love this line of work, but clearly I was not ready for it. I didn't have the guts to do it.

Finally Marshall Simmonds, the man who had been so kind in giving me such a tremendous opportunity, exploded as only a general manager can. He kicked open the door to the control room with his foot and said five words to me, loud and clear: "This is a *communications* business!"

Then he turned and left, slamming the door behind him.

In that instant I leaned forward toward the microphone and said the first words I ever spoke as a broadcaster:

"Good morning. This is my first day ever on the radio. I've always wanted to be on the air. I've been practicing all weekend. Fifteen minutes ago they gave me my new name. I've had a theme song ready to play. But my mouth is dry. I'm nervous. And the general manager just kicked open the door and said, 'This is a communications business.'"

Being able to say at least something gave me the

confidence to go on, and the rest of the show went fine. That was the beginning of my career in talking. I was never nervous on the radio again.

HONESTY

I learned something about talking that morning in Miami Beach, whether you're on the air or off: Be honest. You can never go wrong, in broadcasting or in any area of speech. Arthur Godfrey told me the same thing about how to be a successful broadcaster: Let your listeners and viewers share your experiences and how you feel.

When I made my debut as a television talk show host, also in Miami, I had a similar experience—the only other time I've been nervous on the air since that first day on the radio.

I had never been on TV before, and I let that make me anxious. The producer sat me on a swivel chair. Big mistake. Because of my nerves, I kept swiveling back and forth, and every viewer out there could see it.

It got to be amusing, so I went with my instinct. I put the viewers in my position. I told them I was nervous. I said I had been in radio for three years, but this was my first time on television. And somebody had put me in this swivel chair.

So now everybody knew my situation, and I wasn't nervous anymore. That made me talk better, which made me more successful on that first night in TV, all because I was honest with the people I was talking to.

A person recently asked me, "Suppose you were walking down the hall at NBC News and someone grabbed you, sat you down in a chair in a studio, shoved some papers at you, and said, 'Brokaw's sick. You're on,' and the light came on. What would you do?"

I told them I'd be absolutely honest. I'd look into the camera and say, "I was walking down the hall here at NBC when someone grabbed me, handed me these papers, and said, 'Brokaw's sick. You're on.'"

When I do that, immediately the whole audience knows I've never done news, I don't know what's coming, I'm reading something that's strange to me, I don't know which camera to look at—now the viewers are all in my boat. We're going through this together. They know I've been honest with them, and that I'm going to give them my best effort.

I have successfully communicated to them not only what I'm doing, but the dilemma I'm in, and now I'm in a much better position with them than I would have been if I had tried to fake it. Conversely, if I'm on top of the world and everything is great and I am able to communicate this to my audience, I have them with me for the same reason—I am making them a part of my experience.

THE REST OF THE FORMULA FOR SUCCESS

The right attitude—the *will* to talk even when it might not be comfortable at first—is another basic ingredient

for becoming a better talker. After that fiasco on the radio in Miami, I formed that attitude. When I managed to
survive that case of "mike fright," I made a commitment
to myself that I was going to do two things:
  1. I was going to keep right on talking.
  2. I was going to improve my ability to talk by
      working at it—hard.

     What did I do? Everything. I hosted the morning
show. I did the weather. I filled in as the afternoon sports
reporter. The business report. I anchored the news. I gave
speeches. If somebody called in sick or wanted to take a
day off, I volunteered to work a double shift. I grabbed
every opportunity I could to do as much talking on the
air as possible. My objective was to be on the air and to
be a success at it, so I told myself I was doing just what
Ted Williams did when he felt it was necessary—I was
taking extra batting practice.

     You can take batting practice as a talker, too. In
addition to consulting books and, now, videos on how
to talk, there's a lot you can do yourself. You can talk
out loud to yourself around your house or apartment. I
do. Not often, I hasten to add, but sometimes. I live
alone, so from time to time I'll say a few words off the
cuff or try out something I might want to say later in a
speech or on one of my shows. There's no reason for
me to feel embarrassed about it because there's nobody
else around anyhow. You can do the same thing even if
you don't live alone. You can go into a room by your-

self, or into the basement, or use the time when you're driving your car. And then you can practice simply talking better.

You can also stand in front of a mirror and talk to the image. This is a common technique, especially for people trying to improve their ability as public speakers. But it works for everyday conversation, too. And it helps you to train yourself to make good eye-to-eye contact because you're automatically looking at the image across from you, your reflection in the mirror.

Don't send for the man in the white jacket and the net to come and get me when I tell you this next technique—talking to your dog, or your cat, or your bird, or your goldfish. Pet talk is a great way to practice talking to others—and you don't have to worry about being talked back to or getting interrupted.

Besides the willingness to work on it, you need at least two other ingredients to be a good conversationalist: a sincere *interest in the other person* and an *openness* to them about yourself.

I think it's apparent to viewers of my nightly talk shows on CNN that I'm interested in my guests. I make sure to look them right in the eye. (The failure to do this is the downfall of many people and one we will talk about later.) Then I lean forward on my chair and I ask them a question about themselves.

I respect everyone on my shows—from presidents and Hall of Fame athletes to Kermit the Frog and Miss Piggy of the Muppets, and yes, I've had them on, too.

You cannot talk to people successfully if they think you are not interested in what they have to say or you have no respect for them.

I remember something Will Rogers once said: "Everybody is ignorant, only on different subjects." It's worth remembering this whether you're talking to one person on your way to work or to a TV guest in front of an audience of ten million people. The corollary of this is that everybody is an expert on *something*. Everybody's got at least one subject they love to talk about.

Always respect that expertise. Your listeners will always be able to tell whether you respect them. If they feel you do, they will listen more attentively as you talk. If they don't, nothing you say or do will win them back to what you're talking about.

The remaining ingredient in my formula for success is an openness about yourself while you are talking to others, like my candor with my audience when I developed that severe case of mike fright my first morning on the air. The golden rule—Do unto others as you would have them do unto you—applies to conversation, too. You should be as open and honest with your conversational partners as you'd want them to be with you.

This doesn't mean you should talk about yourself all the time or divulge personal secrets. In fact, just the opposite. Would you want to hear about your neighbor's gallstones? Your co-worker's weekend with her mother-in-law? Probably not, so don't use yours as material for conversation.

At the same time, you *should* be willing to reveal the kind of information that you'd ask of another person. Telling people what your background is, what your likes and dislikes are, is part of the give and take of conversation. It's how we get to know people.

Regis Philbin and Kathie Lee Gifford are good examples of talkers who exhibit an openness about themselves when they are talking to their guests. They come into your room easily and naturally, and they're not afraid to exhibit their tastes or to tell stories on themselves. Without making themselves the focus of their talk, they *are* themselves. They don't try to fake it. If their story or their guest produces a sentimental tone or some other kind of emotion, they are not ashamed to show their feelings. Regis and Kathie Lee obviously know there's nothing wrong with showing a sentimental side if it's a sentimental moment, or fear or sadness or whatever the story or the guest might involve. The audiences in the studio and at home see that and relate to their openness and their obvious genuineness.

Anybody I've ever talked to for more than a few minutes knows at least two things about me: 1) I'm from Brooklyn, and 2) I'm Jewish.

How come they know that about me? Because I share my background with everyone I come in contact with. It's a part of me, deep inside. And I'm proud both of being Jewish and of coming from Brooklyn. So, many of my conversations are dotted with references by me to my background. I enjoy sharing it with people.

If I were a stutterer, I would share that with the person I'm talking to. "It's n-n-nice to m-m-meet you. M-m-my name is Larry King. I have this problem of s-s-stuttering, but I'm happy to talk to you."

Now you've gotten your condition out in the open. You don't have to be afraid to talk to the other person, because you've just shared your situation, which they would find out immediately anyhow, and you've been up front about it, so there is no pretense. The conversation takes on a freedom that will enable both of you to enjoy it more. It won't cure your stuttering, but it will help you be a better talker, while also winning the respect of the person you've started talking to.

Mel Tillis, the country-western singer, takes this approach. He has enjoyed a highly successful singing career and is absolutely charming as a guest in an interview, even though he's a stutterer. It doesn't show up when he's singing, but it does when he's talking. Instead of letting it bother him, Mel is completely up front about it, jokes about it, and is so completely at ease in being himself that he puts you at ease, too.

I had a guest on my TV show in Florida who was born with a cleft palate and spoke in a way that was not at all easy to understand. But he was delighted to be on my show and talk about himself. He was a multimillionaire despite what some people would consider a handicap. Guess what he did to become a multimillionaire? He was a salesman. But he approached anyone he was talking to with no pretense and no attempt to hide the obvious—that he "talked funny." He became successful because he adjusted to his situation and helped others do the same.

2

Breaking the Ice

HOW TO TALK TO STRANGERS

- Overcoming shyness—yours and theirs
- Getting started
- Questions to avoid
- The first rule of conversation
- Body language
- Is anything taboo anymore?

Whether the setting is social or professional, one of the first things to accomplish in talking to people is to put them at ease. Most of us are naturally shy, and believe me, shyness I know. A Jewish kid from Brooklyn who wears glasses knows shy. And all of us tend to be nervous or at least on edge when we're talking to someone we haven't met before or talking in public for the first time.

The best way I've found to overcome shyness is to remind yourself of the old saying that the person you're talking to puts his pants on one leg at a time. Sure it's a cliché, but like most clichés, it happens to be true, which, of course, is why they become clichés in the first place.

That cliché is an effective way of illustrating that we are all human beings, so just because you're talking to a college professor with four degrees or an astronaut who has flown in space at 18,000 miles an hour or someone who has been elected governor of your state doesn't mean you should come unglued.

Always remember this: People you're talking to will enjoy the conversation more if they see you are presenting yourself as someone who's enjoying it, too, whether you consider yourself their equal or not.

Keep in mind that almost all of us started out the same way. Very few of us are born to wealth and power, unless you're a Kennedy or a Rockefeller or a member of one of a few select families. Most of us started out as children of middle- or lower-income families. We worked part-time to pay for college or while getting started in our careers. And chances are the people we're talking to did, too. Maybe we're not as rich and famous as they are or as successful in our field, but we probably came from similar backgrounds, so we can relate as brothers and sisters. You don't have to stand there feeling inferior or intimidated. You belong in that room just as much as the person you're talking to.

It also helps you to overcome your shyness if you remember that the person you're talking to is probably just as shy as you are. Most of us are. Reminding yourself of this will do wonders for your ability to shed your own shyness.

Sometimes you meet a person who's a *lot* shyer than you. I vividly remember the case of an air corps pilot who became an "ace" by shooting down more than five enemy airplanes in World War II.

There is a social organization of such pilots, called simply Aces, with chapters not only in the United States, but in Germany, Japan, Vietnam, and other countries.

All the chapters met in Miami in the late 1960s when I was hosting a nightly radio talk show on station WIOD, then an affiliate of the Mutual Broadcasting System. The *Miami Herald* located the only ace living in Miami, a stocks analyst who had shot down seven German planes in World War II. The paper called my producer and suggested we have him on the air. They said they would include coverage of the show in their feature story about him.

We booked the ace onto the show. He was scheduled for an hour, from eleven to midnight. The paper said it would send a reporter and a photographer.

When our guest arrived in the studio, and I shook hands with him, I noticed his hand was sweaty. I could barely hear him when he said hello. Obviously he was nervous. *Nervous?* Man, this guy was in no condition to fly an airplane.

After five minutes of network news, I opened the hour at 11:05 with a brief background on Aces. Then I asked my first question:

"Why did you volunteer to be a pilot?"

"I don't know."

"Well, obviously you like flying."

"Yeah."

"Do you know *why* you like to fly?"

"No."

A few more questions followed, all answered by our ace in three words or less—Yes. No. I don't know.

I look up at the clock in the studio. It's 11:07, and I'm out of material. I have nothing left to ask this guy. He's scared to death. I mean *terrified*. The *Herald* is embarrassed. I'm not feeling so great myself. Everyone is standing around with the same thought: What are we going to do? We have fifty minutes left. And listeners all over Miami are going to reach for the tuning knobs on their radios any second now.

Again I went with my instinct. I asked him, "If there were five enemy planes overhead and I had a plane parked behind the station, would you go up?"

"Yes."

"Would you be nervous?"

"No."

"Why are you nervous now?"

His answer was, "Because I don't know who's listening."

Then I asked him, "So your fear is of the unknown."

We stopped talking about his air corps days and started talking about fear. His nervousness disappeared. In fact, within ten minutes I had created a monster. Talk about flying? No problem. He's saying with great enthusiasm, "I penetrated the clouds with my plane! I banked sharply to my right! The sun glistened on my wing tip . . ."

They had to carry him out at midnight. He was still talking.

The World War II ace became a good talker because he was able to overcome his fear once he got caught up in the moment and became accustomed to the sound of his voice. At the beginning we were talking about his past, and he didn't know what I was going to ask him. He didn't know what lay ahead in the interview, so he was scared.

But when we started talking about the present, there wasn't anything for him to be scared about. He was talking about what was going on in the studio at the moment, explaining how he felt. As he did that, the nervousness left him and his confidence returned to its normal level. When I could see that, I was able to get him to talk about the past.

You can use the same technique in breaking the ice with someone you're talking to for the first time. How?

Simple—get them on comfortable ground. Ask them about themselves. That will give you something to talk about, and your conversation partner will consider you a fascinating talker. Why? Because people *love* to be talked to about themselves.

Don't take *my* word for it. The same advice comes from Benjamin Disraeli, British novelist, statesman, and prime minister: "Talk to people about themselves and they will listen for hours."

OPENERS

Whether you are at a party or a dinner, on your first day at a new job, meeting your new neighbors, or in any one of a million different settings, the subjects that you can open a conversation with are almost unlimited.

During the 1994 winter Olympics, unless the person you were talking to had just landed from Mars, you could talk about the Tonya Harding–Nancy Kerrigan episode. Mark Twain once complained that everybody talks about the weather but nobody does anything about it, yet the reality is that weather is always a can't miss and completely safe subject for starting a conversation, especially if you know absolutely zero about the other person. Floods in the Midwest, earthquakes, forest fires, and mud slides on the West Coast, and snow and ice in the East provide us with ample openers.

Even though W. C. Fields said, "Any man who hates kids and animals can't be all bad," most people love both, and many have both. Even Fields himself would have agreed that once you learn the person across from you has either kids or pets, you can be off and running, talking to them with the greatest of ease.

Vice President Al Gore is criticized by some for being too stiff, a "wooden" personality on TV, although I have never found him that way. But even those who do would see he is a lively, enthusiastic, and animated person if he's asked about the Baltimore Orioles or his school days at Saint Albans in Washington when his father was a senator from Tennessee. Get him talking about his children, and you'll also see a very warm and human Al Gore.

Any of these subjects would get a conversation with the vice president off to a successful start. Obviously there are many political subjects he could talk about at length. But it's the things that are closest to him personally that make him open up the most. This is true for other people, too.

If you're at a party, the occasion itself is often a starting point for talk. When my friends threw a party for my sixtieth birthday, they called it "the fiftieth anniversary of Larry King's tenth birthday" and gave it a 1940s Brooklyn theme. Lots of conversations that night began with the Dodgers, Coney Island, and other nostalgic topics. Sometimes the setting can give you a conversational wedge. That night the party was held in the historic Decatur House across from the White House, another subject I heard people talking about there.

If you're at a party in someone's home, or even an office, there are likely to be furnishings or mementos that your hosts will cheerfully talk about. Is there a picture of them in Red Square? Ask them about their trip to Russia. Is there a crayon drawing on the wall? Ask which of their children or grandchildren drew it.

AVOID YES/NO QUESTIONS

"Yes/no" questions are the enemy of good talk. By their nature they produce answers of only one or two words:

- "Isn't this hot weather awful?"

- "Do you think we'll have another recession?"

- "Think the Redskins will have another bad year?"

These are all legitimate subjects for good conversations, but if you ask about them in simple yes-or-no terms, that's what you get—yes or no answers. End of topic. And maybe end of conversation.

But, if you couch them in more substantive terms that will generate an expanded answer, the conversation keeps on flowing. The difference:

- "All the hot summers we've been getting make me think there might be something to this business about global warming. What do you think?"

- "The way the stock market has fluctuated so wildly this year, you have to wonder whether our economy is as stable as we like to think. What do you suppose the chances are that we might be headed for another recession?"

- "I've been a Redskins fan ever since I moved to Washington, but I have to admit they have a rebuilding job to do, and the Cowboys are always a threat. What do you think the 'Skins chances are this year?"

The person you're talking to can't get off with only one or two words. The three questions in the second group are on the same subjects as those in the first group, but in each case the question asked the first way might produce only a yes or no. The second way will generate a lengthier answer and, automatically, a better conversation.

THE FIRST RULE OF CONVERSATION: LISTEN

My first rule of conversation is this: I never learn a thing while I'm talking. I realize every morning that nothing *I* say today will teach me anything, so if I'm going to learn a lot today, I'll have to do it by listening.

As obvious as this sounds, you run across proof every day that people simply do not listen. Tell your family or friends your plane will arrive at eight and before the conversation ends they'll ask, "What time did you say your plane is coming in?" And try to estimate the number of times you have heard someone say, "I forgot what you told me."

If you don't listen any better than that to someone, you cannot expect them to listen any better to you. I try to remember the signs you see at railroad crossings in small towns and rural areas: "Stop—Look—Listen." Show the people you talk to that you're interested in what they're saying. They will show you the same.

To be a good talker, you must be a good listener. This is more than just a matter of showing an interest in your conversation partner. Careful listening makes you better able to respond—to be a good talker when it's your turn. Good follow-up questions are the mark of a good conversationalist.

When I watch Barbara Walters's interviews I'm often disappointed, because I think she asks too many "so what" questions, like "If you could come back, what would you like to be?" In my opinion Barbara would be much better if she asked less frivolous questions and better follow-ups, logical extensions of the answer to her previous question. That comes from listening.

I was pleased by something Ted Koppel said to *Time* magazine a few years ago. "Larry listens to his guests," he said. "He pays attention to what they say. Too few interviewers do that." Even though I'm known as a "talking head," I think my success comes first and foremost from listening.

When I interview guests on the air, I make notes ahead of time about the kinds of questions I will ask them. But often I'll hear something in one of their responses that leads me into an unexpected question—and a surprising answer.

Example: When Vice President Dan Quayle was my guest during the 1992 presidential campaign, we talked about the laws governing abortion. He said it made no sense at all for his daughter's school to require his or his wife's permission for their daughter to miss a day of school, but not to get an abortion. As soon as he said that, I was curious about Quayle's personal angle on this political topic. So I asked what his attitude would be if his daughter said she was going to have an abortion. He said he would support her in whatever decision she made.

Quayle's reply made news. Abortion was a white-hot issue in that campaign, and here was President Bush's very conservative running mate, the national Republican spokesman for his conservative wing's unalterable opposition to abortion, suddenly saying he would support his daughter if she decided to have one.

Regardless of your views on that issue, the point here is that I got the response from Quayle because I wasn't just going through a list of questions. I was listening to what he was saying. That was what led me to the newsworthy answer.

The same thing happened when Ross Perot came on my show on February 20, 1992, and denied several times that he was interested in running for president. I kept hearing that his denials were less than complete, and when I put the question differently near the end of the show—bang! Perot said he'd run if his supporters succeeded in registering him on the ballot in all fifty states.

All of that happened not because of what I said, but because of what I *heard*. I was listening.

The late Jim Bishop, the popular writer, columnist, and author, was another New Yorker who spent a lot of time in Miami when I was there. He told me once that one of his pet peeves was people who ask you how you are but then don't listen to your answer. One man in particular was a repeat offender on this subject, so Jim decided to test just how poor a listener this fellow was.

The man called Jim one morning and began the conversation the way he always did: "Jim, how are ya?"

Jim says, "I have lung cancer."

"Wonderful. Say, Jim . . ."

Bishop had proved his point.

Dale Carnegie put it effectively in his book *How to Win Friends and Influence People,* which has now sold fifteen million copies: "To be interesting, be interested."

He added, "Ask questions that other persons will enjoy answering. Encourage them to talk about themselves and their accomplishments. Remember that the people you are talking to are a hundred times more interested in themselves and their wants and problems than they are in you and your problems. A person's toothache means more to that person than a famine in China which kills a million people. A boil on one's neck interests one more than forty earthquakes in Africa. Think of that the next time you start a conversation."

BODY LANGUAGE

The jury is still out on how much you can read into body language, and always will be. Edward Bennett Williams, one of America's most successful lawyers, told me he thought the subject was vastly overrated. His lawyer colleague, Louis Nizer, has just the opposite view: If you cross your legs, you're lying. If you cross your arms, you're uncomfortable. He reads all sorts of messages in your body language and prepares his defendants accordingly, so the judge and jury will get the message from his client's body language that Nizer wants them to.

To me, body language is like spoken language. It's a natural part of conversation and communication. When it comes naturally, it's a terrifically effective form of communication. When it's contrived, it comes across as exactly what it is—fake.

It would be great to have the speaking voice of Sir Laurence Olivier. But if I showed up at work tomorrow trying to talk like the Royal Shakespeare Company, I'd be laughed off the air. For that matter, I'd be so busy trying to think how to pronounce the next sentence that my conversation would be terrible.

Body language works the same way. You can read all the books telling you how to project authority or interest, but if you're striking a pose that isn't natural to you, you will be at best uncomfortable and at worst ridiculous. And if you're uncomfortable, it can actually make you seem insincere when you're not. The body language that you use while you are talking is like the talk itself. Be natural. Speak from the heart.

EYE CONTACT

I've never gone out of my way to study body language, so I don't pretend to be the ultimate authority on it. But there is one rule of body language that you *must* follow for successful conversation: Make eye contact.

Maintaining good eye contact—not just at the beginning and end of your comments, but the whole time you are talking and listening—all go far toward making you a successful talker wherever you are, whatever the occasion might be, and whoever the other person is. I also lean slightly forward toward the person I'm speaking to, to emphasize that I'm focusing on them.

The key, as I've said before, is *listening*. If you are really trying to listen to what's being said, you'll find that it's much easier if you look the other person in the face. In fact, if you are listening closely, most of the appropriate body language will follow automatically. You might nod your head to show an interest in the subject and the person or shake it slightly from side to side in sympathy or incredulity. But again, do this when it feels right; don't just bob your head up and down because you read it in this book.

One further note on this subject: Although it's important to make eye contact frequently as you talk, you don't need to stare continuously in the other person's eyes. Many people would find that uncomfortable, and you might, too. Maintain eye contact when your conversation partner is talking and when you are asking a question. If you're speaking, you can take your eyes off your partner occasionally. However, don't stare off into space as if no one were there. And if you're at a party, *don't* let your eyes wander over your partner's shoulder as if you're looking for someone more important to talk to.

My basic advice on the subject is to worry about how well you're talking and let your body language take care of itself.

WHERE HAVE ALL THE TABOOS GONE?

We don't have to worry nearly as much about taboos as in previous decades and generations. The word *taboo* itself is seldom heard anymore, because so few taboos are left. In the movies, in books, on TV, even in what we used to call "family newspapers," so many restrictions have fallen by the wayside that Cole Porter would have more than enough material for a whole new set of lyrics to his 1920s song "Anything Goes."

Part of the reason is the general permissiveness that set in beginning with the end of World War II and was accelerated in the protest years of the 1960s and 1970s. Another reason comes from my own backyard—cable television. Porter would have trouble believing what you see and hear on some of the cable channels.

Maybe you agree with the tumbling down of these walls of taboos and maybe you don't, but the "almost anything goes" code of life in the United States in the 1990s is here, and it's real. For that reason, although there still are taboos in social conversation, even that kind of talk ain't what it used to be.

That used to be a taboo right there—"ain't." As kids we used to get jumped on every time it soiled our lips. The grown-ups told us firmly and sarcastically, "Ain't ain't in the dictionary." Well, it is now. *Webster's New World Dictionary* says it's a "colloquial word meaning 'am not' . . . a dialectal or substandard contraction for 'is not, are not, has not, and have not.' "

You can even get by with some of what we used to call "cuss words" back in the days when we were shocked to hear Clark Gable as Rhett Butler tell Vivien Leigh as Scarlett O'Hara in *Gone With the Wind*, "Frankly, my dear, I don't give a damn." And I remember the kick we kids got out of standing on the corner in Brooklyn the day after Pearl Harbor and quoting Senator Burton Wheeler of Montana, who lashed out at the Japanese and said, "The only thing to do now is beat hell out of them."

The Bobbitt trial in Virginia early in 1994 resulted in writers and broadcasters mentioning a part of the male anatomy that was never discussed in "proper" mixed company and certainly never brought up in the news media—at least not until only a very few years ago. In that trial the word was always used in a professional context, but that doesn't change the fact that you *never* would have heard it in *any* story of any kind until a very few years ago. You never mentioned the word *condom* except when you were hangin' out with the guys on the corner. Now we have TV commercials about them.

The list of taboo subjects has grown shorter, too, just like the list of taboo words. The proliferation of radio and TV talk shows, all raising subjects never mentioned in living rooms before, has a lot to do with that. There used to be a cliché: "I never discuss religion or politics." When was the last time you heard anybody say that? *Discuss* them? Today we *thrive* on them.

Nonetheless there are still some topics it's best to avoid, either because they are very personal or because people get so emotional about them that they can't discuss them. Even in a wide-open conversation, you wouldn't ask someone, "So, what's your salary?" And with a person you don't know well, you could be tossing a live grenade if you asked, "How do you feel about abortion?"

You have to consider how intimately you know the people you're talking with to decide whether you can break those taboos. With your best friend you might even discuss your salary. In a group that has known each other for years, you might have a frank and illuminating discussion of abortion. But in general, use discretion. Don't presume the person you're talking to will be comfortable with one of those taboo subjects.

A new requirement for being a good talker in our culture is *staying informed*. One of the many profound results of the communications explosions of the last half of the twentieth century is that people know more about what's going on in the world. Before World War II social conversation tended to be less topical than today, simply because people didn't get half as much news and public opinion, and what they did get took a lot longer and came in much smaller doses. Today they may not know more than a few sentences from the evening news, but regardless of how deep their knowledge is, when the Berlin Wall is torn down or Nancy Kerrigan gets whacked across the shin or Frank Sinatra faints on stage, *everybody* knows it, and almost immediately.

To be a successful conversationalist, you have to be ready to talk about what's on people's minds—and it may be the subject they just heard about on the radio and saw on the evening news. Today you have to relate what you're talking about to the interests of the person you're talking to, and they're interested in plenty—because they've heard it on the radio and seen it in the morning paper.

Today the key word in being successful in your social conversation is *relevance*.

3

Social Talk

Social occasions for conversation range from small, comfortable gatherings, like a dinner party among friends, to big, intimidating crowd scenes, like a Washington cocktail party. In between are events like weddings and Bar Mitzvahs. Each one is different, but the principles of conversation are the same: Be open. Find the common ground with your partner. And, always, listen.

COCKTAIL PARTIES

Cocktail parties are a difficult challenge for me. I'm happiest talking with people one on one, so I find a crowd of people in a noisy room a little overwhelming. I don't drink alcohol, and I'm not that big on soft drinks, so I don't have a glass in my hand to use as a prop in conversation. And I tend to fold my arms across my chest, which just happens to be comfortable for me but may make me look less open to starting a conversation.

Instead of being intimidated by the size of the group, look for someone to have a one-on-one conversation with. I try to pick and choose my spots, to start a conversation with someone who looks alert and interested in the goings-on, or else I discreetly join others in conversations already under way that sound interesting.

One trick is not to get caught in the same place for a long period of time. That's where mingling becomes necessary if you are to represent yourself successfully at a cocktail party. Frequently the party will be attended mostly by people you know—neighbors, co-workers, or people who may not work with you but who work in your field. With such a group you should have several topics that will open a conversation.

The Greatest Question of All Time

Remember, asking questions is the secret of good conversation. I'm curious about everything, and if I'm at a cocktail party, I often ask my favorite question: "Why?" If a man tells me that he and his family are moving to another city: "Why?" A woman is changing jobs: "Why?" Someone roots for the Mets: "Why?"

On my television show, I probably use this word more than any other. It's the greatest question ever asked, and it always will be. And it is certainly the surest way of keeping a conversation lively and interesting.

How to Get out of a Conversation

If you find yourself stuck with a real bore, or simply feel it's time to end a long conversation and move on, there's always one guaranteed way to get out of the conversation: "Excuse me. I have to visit the restroom." If you make it sound urgent enough, no one will take offense at your departure. When you come back, you start another conversation, only this time with someone else.

Or, if you spot someone you know nearby, you can make your escape with, "Stacey! Have you met Bill?" As Stacey is shaking hands with Bill, you can say, "I'll be back in a minute, but I know you two will have a lot to talk about." At a busy cocktail party they won't be surprised if you don't come back in a minute. Of course, if your first conversation partner is a killing bore, Stacey may never forgive you, so use this technique with caution.

Other good exit lines:

1. "This food is delicious. I'm going to go help myself to seconds."
2. "Would you excuse me? I'm going to go say hello to our host." (Or "... to a friend I haven't seen in a while.")
3. "Well, I guess I'd better go and mingle some more."

It's important not to make too much of your exit. Don't spend the minute beforehand glancing around the room desperately or be too apologetic. Just wait for a slight pause, say something polite, and move on as if it's a natural thing to do. Simply saying "It was nice talking to you" and turning away can be graceful enough, as long as you sound as though you actually did enjoy the conversation.

SMALL DINNERS

Making conversation at a small dinner always comes easier for me. I think a lot of people feel this way. Usually, at this kind of party, the guests know each other or at least are there because of something they have in common. You have more choices and more techniques available to you in talking to others and getting them to talk to you.

I like to control such settings. That doesn't mean I

dominate the conversation at the table. Quite the contrary: it means I can direct the flow of the talk, making it go where I want it to, cover what subjects I want it to, and involve the guests I want it to, all to make sure the guests are enjoying themselves. But I have to do it in such a way that everyone around my part of the table will be interested in the conversation. Especially at this kind of event, it's essential to listen to what everybody says.

Even then there are certain things you can't control—somebody had too much to drink before dinner, another guest had a terrible day at the office. Someone has a serious illness in the family and doesn't really feel up to a whole lot of conversation tonight. The best you can do is steer the conversation away from those people and let others do more of the talking. It also helps if you can find a lighthearted subject that may take their minds off their own problems.

Outside of those exceptions, I can usually help to make the evening enjoyable and successful for all parties concerned. "Quarterbacking" a conversation is a skill I've been able to develop over the years in my profession. But even if you're not a professional talker, you can do it, too. Here are some tips.

HOW TO QUARTERBACK A CONVERSATION

Choose a Topic That Will Involve Everybody

I'll talk more about what-ifs later; these are hypothetical questions that all the guests will have an opinion about.

It's better to start with something like that than with a heavy-duty topic like politics.

Try to avoid topics that only some of the guests are going to be expert in, or the nonexperts will be shut out. The obvious example is shop talk. If four couples are at a dinner party, and four of the spouses all work in the same law firm, once they start talking about the office it can be excruciating for the poor husbands and wives who don't know, or care, about the firm's daily affairs.

Solicit Opinions

Don't just offer your own opinions. You'll be remembered as a better conversationalist if you ask the opinions of others around you. Henry Kissinger, another person who's good at controlling things because he's done it all his life, is a great one at this. Even on a subject on which he's an expert—and you can imagine there are a lot of them—he will often turn and ask, "What do you think?"

Help the Shyest Person in the Group

I'm always aware of the need to keep the guests on both sides of me participating in the table talk, especially those who don't seem to be joining in. If the person on my left seems on the shy side but the guest on my right is outgoing and enthusiastic, I make a special attempt to bring the one on my left into things. I nod to them as if seeking their agreement on what's being said. I apply the Kissinger method: "What do you think?" Suddenly the shy person is involved in the conversation.

Another idea is to segue to a topic that you know that person will talk about. If the conversation is about education, you can say, "That reminds me, your daughter is at Washington High. How's she liking it?"

Don't Monopolize the Conversation

A serious danger in social talk is to go on so long that you monopolize the conversation, turning yourself from a gifted conversationalist into a bore. Give those you talk to a chance to talk back—equal time, as we say in broadcasting. And don't feel that you have to cross every *t* and dot every *i* by including every detail of a story you're telling. That's what people do after telling you, "To make a long story short . . ." When you hear that, get ready for a long story. Keep your own stories brief; the more people there are in your conversational group, the briefer they should be.

"Overtalk"—my term—does not make a favorable impression on your listener. If anything, it hurts the impression you are making. People who talk too much, in the opinion of others, pay a price and lose a certain degree of credibility. Instead you want to be known as someone who follows the age-old advice of show business: Know when to get off stage.

Don't Give Your Partner the Third Degree

At a reception, a dinner, or in a similar setting, one of the tricks is to remember you are not writing a book. You do not have to find out everything humanly possible about the person you're talking to or every detail of the experience being discussed. After all, you are only spending a short time in conversation with him or her, a couple of hours at most if it's a dinner, and even then you're not expected to be talking every minute of the time. Just as you shouldn't be a monologuist, neither should you be an interrogator. There will not be a quiz after the evening is over.

The other extreme may be just as bad—being so short on words that people think either you're not bright enough to say much or you're an unfriendly person.

"What If?"

"What if" questions are a can't miss way of starting a conversation in a social setting or picking it up during a lull:

- "What if North Korea keeps on stonewalling the UN on inspecting its nuclear plants. Think we'll have another Korean War?"

- "So Barry Switzer is the new coach of the Dallas Cowboys. What if they have two bad

years in a row under him. Would Jerry Jones
fire him?"

- "What if you had just built your dream
  house in California, and you were told sci-
  entists had suddenly discovered an earthquake zone in the area. Would you move?"

The number and type of what-if questions is without limit. And you can always think of one related to
something that's in the news and on people's minds at the
moment.

Moral and philosophical what-ifs are just as effective as topical ones like those. A good what-if is one that
appeals to everyone, one that cuts across generational,
educational, and sociological lines.

Here's a question I have often asked at dinner
parties:

You're on an island with only one other person,
your best friend. He's dying of cancer. In his final days he
tells you, "I have one hundred thousand dollars in a bank
back home. When I die, make sure my son goes to medical school." Then he dies. But his son is a no-good play-
boy who has no intention of going to med school and will
waste that hundred grand away in a couple of months.
But *your* son is entering college, and he has a burning
desire to become a doctor. Which one do you give the
money to for medical school?

•   •   •

I've asked this question of everyone from the president of Yale to a twenty-two-year-old rookie with the St. Louis Cardinals, and it has never failed to get a conversation going. Everyone has an opinion, most of them different, all of them legitimate. Sometimes this one topic of conversation lasts the whole evening.

An organization called Mensa, composed of some of the world's greatest intellects—men and women in the top 2 percent in intelligence—likes to have its members consider questions like these at great length as a means of encouraging greater thought and discussion on the moral dimension in our lives as human beings.

Here are two of theirs:

There are four men in a mine when the mine caves in. They try to escape through the only hole to the surface. They are stacked up on top of each other, but the one on top is an obese person. Just as he gets halfway out of the hole, he gets stuck. The three men stacked below start to run out of air. Should they shoot him and pull him out of the way? Or should they let him keep struggling, knowing they probably will suffocate below him? Who should live—the one or the three?

Should someone who was given the power to become invisible feel compelled to obey conventional moral codes? I was at a Mensa meeting when this was the topic of discussion. Many people said they would obey the same rules of behavior, from the Ten Commandments to their own morals, that they have always followed. But not everybody. One man said he would take advantage of his invisibility to sit in on business negotiations, then make investments that would bring him a killing in the stock market. Another said he would hang around jockeys, get as much information as he could, and bet a bundle at the races. Others admitted they would hatch similar schemes. Invisibility would give you the ultimate power. You could rule the world. If *you* were given the ability to make yourself invisible, what would you do with it?

Maybe these will give you ideas for philosophical what-ifs. And by all means make up your own as you go. Don't feel you have to refer to a list.

If conversation is flowing right along, forget the what-if question. Who needs it? *But* if the talk starts to drag and sputter, and threatens to stall out altogether, then you wheel in a what-if as a means of reviving things.

By the way, every so often you may try a what-if that *doesn't* seem to strike a spark with the group you're talking to. If you've picked a good question, that probably won't happen. But suppose this group just got out of a monastery and never heard of your subject, or maybe it just happens to hit too close to home for them to take it lightly. (Suppose the person's mother actually *got* trapped in a cave. That kind of conversational bad luck strikes from time to time.) Don't push it. If your hypothetical question doesn't get talk going spontaneously, you can't do it by forcing it. The best thing to do is either move on to a completely different what-if or shift gears and move on to another kind of subject. If that doesn't work, the group is a dud, not the question. At that point you're allowed to give up. Start floating to another spot in the room and another conversation.

Pay Attention to the Physical Setting

Experienced hosts who thrive on entertaining guests make an art, almost a science, out of arrangements for the evening, concerning themselves with everything from the color of the flowers to the arrangement of the furniture. I'm no expert on flowers and I'm not an interior designer, but I can tell you something about the sets CNN uses on *Larry King Live* and why my show looks the way it does.

The desk that my guests and I sit at in Washington was designed by CNN's professionals in Atlanta. It is intended to create a feeling of comfort and intimacy. And it works. I feel that way on the set, and most of the guests do, too. Notice we don't have a table with flowers. We don't have any overpowering pictures of Washington scenes. We just have the desk and a map on the wall behind the guest. The set has a sweep to it, giving it an air of wide coverage, which is exactly what CNN provides and is known for. The set implies the drama and excitement that we want our viewers to feel. If they feel it, they'll stay tuned, and they'll tune in again tomorrow night at nine eastern time.

That set has remained the same since we went on the air in 1985, except that we expanded the map to increase that feeling of sweeping worldwide coverage. The only difference between our set in Washington and the one we use when I'm in New York is the backdrop. In New York, viewers see the evening Manhattan skyline behind the guest. Everything else is the same but slightly smaller.

On both our Washington and New York sets, our guests comment frequently about the familiarity of the surroundings. They tell us the environment feels like something they're used to. When I have more than one guest at the same time, they remark about how close they are sitting to each other. But that closeness works. It produces an atmosphere of intimacy, the feeling that the two guests and I are having this private-but-public conversation and the viewer is sitting in on it.

Unfortunately you can't hold all your intimate dinner parties on the set of *Larry King Live*. But you could take a leaf from our book. First, the setting doesn't have to be fancy or dramatic, as long as it gives your guests a feeling of comfort. If you have a beautiful garden, but the weatherman says it'll be forty degrees tonight, don't serve dinner out there. Second, obvious as it sounds, allow people to sit close together. If you're having four people to dinner, don't use your grandmother's gigantic table that seats twelve. Even if that's the only table you have, it's better to use it as a buffet and eat from your laps in the living room. Nothing makes people feel more awkward during a meal than an underpopulated table.

Talk Between the Sexes

Talk between the sexes, especially between two people who have just met, may be the hardest form of talking. It is for me.

The way you strike up a conversation with someone of the opposite sex is very different now from when I was growing up. In those days a guy might walk up to a woman at a cocktail party and say: "What's a nice girl like you doing in a place like this?" Or: "Where have you been all my life?" Or: "Haven't I seen you someplace before?"

Lines like that don't work anymore. In fact, the idea of "lines" seems like a cliché today. If you start off with one of those I just quoted, you'll sound as if you're auditioning for the part of a lounge lizard.

This is not just a problem for men, of course. For women, too, knowing how to get started talking with a man is difficult. In fact, it's extra difficult for some women, because for so long it was taboo for a woman to approach a man at all. It was okay to initiate small talk at a tea party, but for a single woman to imply to a man that she found him attractive was, at best, "forward," at worst, brazen.

When I was dating in high school and into my twenties and thirties, it was a serious no-no for a girl even to call a boy, or a woman to call a man, on the telephone. It just wasn't done. Your parents would tell you, "Nice girls don't call boys. The boys call *them*." But they didn't really have to tell you that. The girls wouldn't call you anyhow.

In those days a strict unwritten code governed how young men and women behaved toward each other. Members of the opposite sex never gave each other clothes as gifts, not even a sweater. Well, maybe a necktie or a pair of gloves. Anything else was considered much too personal. A good book. A nice wallet. Nothing more intimate than that. Young men and women certainly never took overnight trips to the beach or anywhere else, even with their "steadies." And, the code said, don't call *him*. He's supposed to call *you*.

Today all those taboos are history. If a man is trying to get a woman on the phone, he doesn't have to keep calling back. If she's out of her office and he can't reach her, she can always call him from her courtroom or her client's office or from her airplane on her way to San Francisco. And if a woman sees a man she'd like to get to know, she can make the first move.

The flip side of the change is that women can now agonize just as much as men about how to open a conversation.

Arthur Godfrey's advice to me—"Be yourself"—may fit here better than in any other category of talking. My suggestion on how to talk to a member of the opposite sex for the first time, one you'd like to see more of, is simply to be candid.

In my case, being candid would mean saying, "I'm not really good at this. I don't strike up a conversation very well with a woman I've just met. But I'd enjoy talking to you for a few minutes. My name is Larry King."

If she responds, you've got a conversation. If she doesn't, you're off the hook, because you know a conversation with her isn't going anywhere anyhow.

Here's another approach that I might use. Suppose I meet a woman at a small private dinner; I might say, "You know, there really aren't any gimmicks for a man to start a conversation with a woman anymore. I can think of all those lines that men used to use to strike up a conversation with a woman he's just met, but they don't work anymore. So how can we start talking to each other?"

From a candid opening you can proceed to the next step—getting a feel for the other person's interests, so you can decide if you want to continue the conversation. You do it simply by mentioning a subject of interest to you:

- "Well, everybody seems to have an opinion about the verdict in the Menendez trial. What's yours?"

- "I just heard on the car radio coming over here that the stock market dropped another

fifty-eight points today. Do you think we're
headed for another October 1987?"

Questions like these serve two purposes. They give
you a follow-up subject to talk about after you've just
introduced yourselves to each other, and they are a gauge
of the intelligence and interests of the other person.

If the man you're talking to responds to the first
question by saying, "I was shocked to hear that verdict,"
that tells you he probably follows current events, is able
to hold up his end of a conversation, and may have some
things in common with you.

But if he says, "Oh, I don't know anything about
that," he's telling you the exact opposite, which may
mean you should look around for someone who's closer
to your wavelength.

Or if you're talking to a woman and she responds to
the question about the stock market by saying, "Oh, no.
There was an article about that in the *Wall Street Journal*
today," you know you've connected.

But if she says, "I never follow that stuff. It's so
boring," chances are you may find her boring, too, and
vice versa.

My advice in meeting people, and especially in talk
between the sexes, is to learn as much as you can about
the other person as early in the conversation as possible.
Engage them in areas that you're interested in and stick
to your natural conversational style. If you're a witty,
bantering sort of talker, see if she is, too. If you're a

woman who's on the serious side, see if he is. If you like politics or sports or movies, or all of the above, see if your partner does.

If he or she isn't interested in the subjects that interest you, excuse yourself politely. Then move on. There's bound to be someone else in the room who's more fun for you to talk to.

FAMILY GATHERINGS, FROM WEDDINGS TO FUNERALS

Weddings and Bar Mitzvahs (Bas Mitzvahs for the young women now, something we didn't have when I was growing up) or birthday parties and holiday get-togethers are usually comfortable settings for talking. Most of the people there know each other, and the occasions are happy and relaxed, except during those interminable time-outs when we're waiting for the photographer to finish taking a zillion shots of the wedding party.

Even with people you haven't met before, you have ready-made subjects for conversation at this kind of gathering.

"Do you know the bride? I haven't met the groom before, but I'm an old friend of the bride's. She's lovely, and what a nice family she has!" You can do a half hour just on the bride or the groom.

The person you're talking to knows the other half of the wedding party? Same thing. Now you *and* the person you're talking to can *each* do a half hour.

"Do you know where they're going on their honeymoon?" If you or your conversation partner has been there, too, you're set for another half hour.

Funerals, naturally, can be a challenge. I find them one of the most difficult settings for making social talk. I have one basic rule in speaking to members of the family at a wake or funeral: Don't be so obvious as to be redundant. One of the most frequently heard comments at a funeral is "I know how you must feel." I avoid that statement, for two reasons. First, if the death was caused by natural, normal circumstances—in other words, the same unfortunate kind of loss that all of us over the age of twelve have already gone through from time to time—the bereaved is already aware that we know how they feel. Second, if the circumstances of the death were truly unusual or violent or shocking for some other reason, then there's no way in the *world* we could know how they feel.

Similarly, comments such as "This is such a tragedy" or "It's a terrible loss" imply that the level of their grief is yours to gauge, which it's not.

It's better to speak for yourself and to be sympathetic but not dolorous. I often tell family members at a wake or funeral about a favorite memory of mine involving the deceased: "I'll never forget when I was in the hospital and John took the time to come over and see me on a Friday night, even though it was raining cats and dogs and he had just gotten home from New York."

If you know the family reasonably well, it can help

to recall something humorous. "Did you know Fritz played the greatest practical joke that anyone ever did to me?"

It's a light comment in a setting where one is badly needed, it's a personal story unique to you, and it's something the family may not have heard about its departed member.

If you didn't know the person who died, you can make a brief comment about his or her accomplishments—how respected they were in their career, what a good family man he was, how well she did during her terms on the city council. And you don't have to hire a consultant to come up with ideas for you in a situation like this. Just ask yourself what you would like to hear if you were a member of the grieving family. Usually it's best to keep it simple. At a time like this, frankly, the family is not going to be concerned with how good a conversationalist you are. If you say it sincerely, "I'm sorry—we'll really miss her" can be enough.

If you're a speaker at a funeral, the same rules of consideration apply, in my opinion. I'm not an expert on this, but I can offer an example from my own experience.

In November of 1993, my dear friend and my agent, Bob Woolf, passed away unexpectedly. To be Bob's client was also to be his friend, because that's just the kind of a human being he was. He and his talented daughter, Stacey Woolf, have represented me for years, always with integrity—that always came first with Bob—respect, success, politeness, and good humor. They represented all their other clients the same way, from Larry Bird and Carl Yastrzemski to Gene Shalit and Pete Axthelm. It hit all of us hard when we got the stunning news that Bob had died in his sleep in Florida one autumn afternoon, only a few days after emceeing my sixtieth birthday party in Washington.

When Stacey asked me to be one of five speakers at her father's funeral, I was both honored and uncertain, honored to be selected but uncertain as to what to say. The circumstances are so emotional that a speaker wants to be extra careful to pick exactly the right subject and express himself in precisely the right words. I decided, as I usually do, to go with my instinct, and my instinct in this case told me to keep it light.

I was the last speaker. The other four were all good, especially Bob's rabbi, and then it was my turn. It was the hardest speech I've given in my life. In fact, it wasn't really a speech; it was a sharing of feelings and memories with others who were going through the same grieving process that I was.

I stood there with the closed casket holding my friend near me. I found it a wrenching moment, but then I remembered it was a wrenching time for Stacey and her family and for many other people there, too, so I began to talk:

"I was the other Larry among Bob's clients. When Larry Bird and I called in at the same time, guess who got put on hold."

That line produced the first real laugh of the day,

and you could tell it came from relief as much as from humor. I knew the people in the congregation wanted to laugh. Bob was a happy man. He enjoyed being around people. And he enjoyed laughing with them. So I continued speaking:

"You know, Bob loved to take pictures. He was always snapping something. Mel Brooks's two thousand-year-old man said the greatest inventions in the history of the world were Liquid Prell and Saran Wrap. But if you asked Bob the same question, he'd have said twenty-four-hour photo processing."

Again my listeners took comfort in the humor. I felt that my instinct had been right, that the others at the funeral felt I had chosen an appropriate way to speak about Bob. In difficult situations like funerals, I recommend listening to your instinct. It has a talent for telling you what to say and what *not* to say. If you have a feeling that others would want to hear a particular memory or a certain quotation, you're probably right. By the same token, if a remark pops into your mind but you have a gnawing fear that it might be taken the wrong way, hold it back.

I found talking at Bob's funeral a very difficult thing to do, and I'm sure the other speakers did, too. But all five of us spoke that day for the same reason—because it was the right thing to do and the best way any of us could pay tribute to our departed friend.

That, after all, is what wakes and funerals are for.

Nobody enjoys them. But you're all there for the same reason—because you loved the person and you want to do the right thing. Nobody came to Bob Woolf's funeral to hear Larry King speak. We came, all of us, because it was Bob and because we owed him our best good-bye.

That would be my advice to you if you ever find yourself in the position of being invited to speak at a funeral. Remember that people did not come to hear you speak. They came for the same reason you did—to mourn the passing of a loved one and to celebrate his or her life among you. Show respect and affection for the deceased. Show compassion for the family. Keep it short. And a chuckle or two won't hurt.

HOW TO TALK TO CELEBRITIES

Talking to celebrities is another problem for many people. No matter how down-to-earth a celebrity might be, it's easy to be intimidated by his or her fame.

If you're not careful, you can embarrass yourself, sometimes without ever knowing it. Movie actors, TV stars, athletes, and others tell stories about all kinds of experiences where people innocently and unknowingly put their foot in it.

One of the standards is, "Oh, I've been a big fan of yours since I was a little kid." Ballplayers hear this one so often, they use it to kid each other: "My father used to take me to see you play." Whether you mean it or not, these remarks tell the celebrities that they're old.

Another standard comment: "I've always thought I could have been a major-league baseball player [or movie star or novelist]." This belittles the accomplishments of the person you're talking to and suggests that, hell, anybody could have done the same.

On my show I have talked to celebrities from every field I can think of, and I can promise you, they enjoy a normal conversation just as much as you and I do. I approach them not as famous people, just as people—who probably have the same likes, dislikes, and feelings as the rest of us. And I'm usually successful in getting them to talk by using exactly the same techniques I've been mentioning here.

A common mistake in talking to celebrities is to stereotype them as people who don't know anything about anything else except their professions. The movie business and the athletic world are full of intelligent, educated, informed men and women who are interested in, and involved in, a wide variety of activities and causes, yet they are asked only about acting or sports. If you happen to know about the celebrity's "extracurricular" interest, you might find she'll speak to you about it much more freely than she would about her professional life. For example, ask Woody Allen about the New York Knicks basketball team, or Paul Newman about his charity work with kids.

If you allow yourself to be intimidated by the celebrity's fame, you're flirting with disaster—like the small-town mayor who was introducing Walter Pidgeon, one of the most famous movie stars in the world, at a war bond rally during World War II.

"Mr. Privilege," the mayor said to the audience, "this is indeed a pigeon."

4

Eight Things the Best Talkers Have in Common

**SUCCESSFUL PEOPLE ARE SUCCESSFUL
TALKERS, AND VICE VERSA**

- **What they have in common**
- **Learning from Frank Sinatra, Bill Clinton, and Edward Bennett Williams**

Most successful people are successful talkers. Not surprisingly, the reverse is also true. If you have developed the ability—and it *can* be developed—to talk well, you will be successful. If you feel that you're a successful person already, you can make yourself even more successful by making yourself a better talker.

Successful people who cannot express themselves

well? I can't think of one. Zero. Maybe they're not good at small talk. Or maybe they're not good public speakers. But they speak well enough, in enough different settings, to achieve success and even greatness.

Nobody ever called Harry Truman a great orator, but many have called him a great president. One reason was that he was a good talker in political give-and-take. And although he was not a spellbinding speaker, he *was* a good communicator in his determination to make himself clearly understood. Instead of soaring rhetoric, he put his ideas into plain, down-to-earth English. No one has ever summed up the responsibility of a president better than Truman's simple phrase: "The buck stops here." That's being a good talker.

Lyndon Johnson, like Truman, was an indifferent speaker, but nobody was his equal when he was talking to you while grabbing your lapels in the Senate cloakroom.

Martin Luther King Jr. was successful for reasons exactly the opposite of Truman and Johnson. He was a masterful public speaker—a spellbinder who could and did arouse an entire nation with his unequaled ability to talk into a microphone on a stage.

I'll talk more about public speaking in a later chapter. For most of us, the biggest concern is being effective in everyday conversation, whether it's in social settings or in business. Thinking back over all the people I've talked to, on or off the air, I've noticed that the best conversationalists have several things in common.

WHAT THE BEST TALKERS HAVE IN COMMON

- They *look at things from a new angle,* taking unexpected points of view on familiar subjects.

- They *have broad horizons.* They think about, and talk about, a wide range of issues and experiences beyond their own daily lives.

- They are *enthusiastic,* displaying a passion for what they're doing with their lives and an interest in what you're saying to them at that moment.

- They *don't talk about themselves all the time.*

- They are *curious.* They ask "Why?" They want to know more about what you're telling them.

- They *empathize.* They try to put themselves in your place, to relate to what you're saying.

- They have a *sense of humor.* And they don't mind using it on themselves. In fact, the best conversationalists frequently tell stories on themselves.

- They have their own *style* of talking.

LOOKING AT THINGS FROM A NEW ANGLE

The first common characteristic in that list may be the most frequently found ingredient in people who talk successfully. Frank Sinatra is an example. Frank is a great dinner guest. He's interested in everything. And if you're lucky enough to get him talking about his profession, he is fascinating, not because he tells you what a great star he is (because he doesn't), but because of the depth of his knowledge about music. He has thought so much about his craft that he often comes up with new, unexpected insights into it.

One night a few years ago, I was sitting next to Frank at a private dinner honoring Irving Berlin in California. He had been asked to sing one of Berlin's classics ("Remember?") after dinner. That was a big hit when I was growing up. People my age and older remember it as a soft, tender love song, a romantic tribute to a person's sweetheart.

But Frank surprised me. "I used to sing that song a lot," he said. "I always sang it as a gentle ballad. But tonight I'm going to sing it in a different way. You know why? Because that's a bitter song."

I thought about it for a second. Then we started reciting the lyric:

> *Remember the night?*
> *The night you said, "I love you."*
> *Remember?*
>
> *Remember you vowed*
> *By all the stars above you.*
> *Remember?*

Frank said, "That guy's angry. So I'm going to sing it in a different style tonight, with an edge to it." He did, and he showed that he is a genius at interpreting a song as well as singing it.

Sinatra was able to enliven our dinner conversation because he *took a new angle* on an old subject, in this case a familiar song. He approached it that night in a way that no other singer had ever thought of. Every time I've heard that song since, I've heard it in a different way, because of what Frank said. Now *that's* a good conversationalist.

BROADEN YOUR HORIZONS

Governor Mario Cuomo of New York is another delightful dinner companion, but his son, Andrew, is just as entertaining. Cuomo will not only agree with me on this—he'll tell you why.

Andrew Cuomo, who is in his thirties, is an assistant secretary of housing and urban development in the Clinton administration. He gave up a promising law career in private practice to go to Washington to serve in the Clinton administration and do his part in the field of public service. He is a sophisticated, well-rounded person, both interest*ing* and interest*ed*, as Dale Carnegie might say.

I told the governor over the phone one day recently how much I enjoy talking to Andrew when I run into him from time to time in Washington and what a well-rounded young man I found him to be. Then Cuomo senior told me there was a reason for that, an advantage that few of us have, and Andrew was alert enough to reap the full advantage of it.

Governor Cuomo said: "All four of Andrew's grandparents lived until he was thirty. Two of them are still living."

Andrew, his father explained, was always kind and thoughtful toward his grandparents. He talked to them. Asked them questions. Listened to their experiences. These were four elderly people from two sections of Italy, born at the start of the twentieth century, when people traveled by horse and cart, with no electric light, no radio, when diseases that have long since been eradicated were killers and family members and neighbors never made it past the first few grades in school and news from outside the village reached them by word of mouth.

It's not that Andrew Cuomo is a fountain of information about life in the old country and is therefore a charming guest on the subject of Italy. The point is that Andrew grew up *listening* to the people around him and continues that practice to this day. As a result, he is a well-rounded conversationalist because of what he has learned on a wide range of subjects, and his habit of listening makes him an enjoyable person to talk to.

When Governor Cuomo made this point to me, he got me to thinking. There's a saying that you broaden your horizons through travel, but if you are curious enough to listen to other people, you can broaden your horizons without leaving your backyard. All of us had grandparents. Maybe they didn't live as long as Andrew's, but chances are all of us have known people who lived well into their eighties or even their nineties, some past a hundred. And we've probably soaked up information and stories and impressions from them that we don't even realize.

After my father died, my mother was able to get an elderly woman to help care for us while Mom tried to scrape up enough money for us to eat and have clothes to wear and be able to keep our little apartment in Brooklyn's Bensonhurst neighborhood. The woman helper was in her eighties. Her father fought for the Union Army in the Civil War. As a child, she actually *saw* Abraham Lincoln. And I was able to talk to her.

So, in a way, my childhood in Brooklyn was a window onto another era in American history. You might have the same kind of knowledge from your years with your elders. There are all kinds of places it might fit into conversation—whether the talk is of health care, grandparents, teachers, coaches, or the Civil War.

The moral of the story is this: Remember your grandparents and other elderly people from your earlier years, your experiences with them and their stories and insights. They—and other people with backgrounds different from your own—can help you broaden your conversational repertoire and broaden your thinking.

ENTHUSIASM

I think one reason I've had a certain amount of success in broadcasting is that the audience can see that I love what I'm doing. You can't fake that, and if you try, you fail. If you really do love what you're doing and project that enthusiasm to the people you're talking to, your chances for success become greater. I've seen this with people with careers as diverse as those of President Clinton and Tommy Lasorda.

Lasorda, the manager of the Los Angeles Dodgers, came on my radio show the night after his team suffered a crushing loss to Houston in the National League playoffs in 1981. From his performance and enthusiasm, you never would have guessed that he was the *losing* manager. When I asked him how he could be so exuberant, he said, "The best day of my life is when I manage a winning game. And the second best day of my life is when I manage a losing game."

President Clinton, whom I interviewed on the anniversary of his first year in the White House, said almost the same thing about being president. Both Bill Clinton and Tommy Lasorda are good talkers—and ones I love to have on my show—because of what they have in common: they have great enthusiasm for their jobs, and they communicate it in their talk. That enthusiasm, and their willingness to share it, has obviously made them not just successful as talkers, but successful in their chosen careers.

Maybe you don't have the same kind of enthusiasm for your job as Tommy Lasorda. I hope you do, but not everyone is so lucky. Then think of the things you *are* enthusiastic about: your kids, your hobbies, a charity you work with, even a book you've just read. Without making it into a hobbyhorse, draw on that enthusiasm in your conversation. If you can take a subject you're passionate about, and make your listener understand why, you'll be an interesting talker.

DON'T JUST TALK ABOUT YOURSELF

To hold up your end of the conversation, you obviously have to tell your partner something about yourself and answer questions he or she may ask. But don't go on too long. Instead, turn the conversation around, as in "How about *you*, Mary? Where do *you* work?"

BE CURIOUS

The best conversationalists are curious about everything. That's why they are good at listening and why they have broad horizons—they're always learning something new.

SHOW EMPATHY

The people we most enjoy talking to are ones who show empathy for us—who make clear they relate to what we're *feeling* as well as what we're saying. When you tell someone you've got a new job, you'd like them to say "Wow! That's great!" not just "Oh, really?" So do the same when you are the listener in a conversation.

Oprah Winfrey, to take a talker we're familiar with from television, makes a strong connection with her viewers because she so clearly empathizes with the guests on her show. You can tell immediately that she really cares about what they're saying and is relating to it. Her empathy also helps to draw out her guests and get them to be open with her. It's another mark of a good conversationalist.

All the best conversationalists among TV show hosts share this quality. I call them "the commiserators." If you told them you had a brain tumor—or just chicken pox—they would exhibit empathy and support for you and project that to the audience. Sonya Friedman, who

hosts *Sonya Live* on CNN every weekday, is another
good example.

Dick Cavett is another great commiserator, a man
of obvious intelligence and broad interests whose style
shows he's interested in his guest and how the guest feels,
rather than in probing for something sensational.

SHOW YOUR SENSE OF HUMOR

Humor is as welcome in conversation as it is anywhere
else, and sometimes it's much more critically needed.
When I'm giving a speech, one of my own cardinal rules
is "Never stay too serious too long." That same applies
to conversation, maybe more so.

But humor, like anything else, doesn't work if it's
forced. The best humorists and comics know this and
don't try. The best example who comes to mind is Bob
Hope.

Bob never tries to be unusually funny as a dinner
guest. He's certainly not boring or solemn, but he's sophisticated enough not to try to do his old vaudeville
monologues at the dinner table. Everybody already
knows he's funny on stage, on TV, and in the movies, so
he doesn't have to prove it. Furthermore, Hope is more
than a comedian and entertainer. He's also a successful
businessman who is interested in many things in this
world and a patriotic American who has performed all
over the world for members of our armed forces. His
experiences in all these areas give him plenty to talk about

and make him a lively conversation partner, even if he doesn't rattle off one-liners.

Al Pacino has a different natural style of humor. He's one of America's finest dramatic actors, but off screen he's a funny guy: New York funny. He has that New Yorker's reaction to things, the ability to shrug off so many of life's threats and dangers because New Yorkers are surrounded by threats and dangers all the time right in their own hometown.

We were standing with Walter Cronkite, Pelé, and others in the lobby of the Beverly Wilshire Hotel in Los Angeles only a few hours after the terrible earthquake in January 1994. We were in town for a cable TV awards banquet the night before. So the four or five of us are talking to each other, each telling about his own reaction when the quake hit. All of us are shaken—at least I am. But Pacino shrugs and says, "I'm from New York. I thought it was a bomb." It wasn't a joke, just a deadpan comment, but at that moment it broke us up.

Someone with a very different style is George Burns. George is exactly what you see on television. He can't be any other way but funny, and for him, it's natural to draw on his lifetime collection of gag lines in his conversation.

For example, suppose the conversation at a party turns to health care, and everyone is weighing in with deep thoughts about managed competition and the like. But somebody asks George, who will soon be one hundred years old, what he thinks about doctors today. He

says: "I smoke ten cigars a day, and I have two double
martinis every day at lunch and two more at dinner. And
I run around with women much younger than I am. People ask me what my doctor thinks of this."

Then he looks around the table and says matter-of-
factly, "My doctor died ten years ago."

That's George Burns just being George Burns. Nobody gets turned off by it just because he's using some of
his routine. His routine is himself, and all of us know it.
Instead of being bored, the guests at his table are
charmed.

However, it also works because he didn't force it
into the conversation. His was just a natural follow-up
comment to what they were saying about doctors. If he
were to say to the guests around him, "Hey! Lemme tell
you this funny line that I use in my routine," it would be
a turnoff because he'd be trying too hard and because it
would break the flow of conversation.

That's an important point to remember about humor. Whatever your style of humor is, let it come into the
conversation naturally. Professional comedians know
that timing is everything, and bringing everything to a
halt so you can tell your gag is bad timing. Even if you
heard a hilarious joke today at the office, don't interrupt
a conversation in progress just so you can tell it.

Don Rickles is another guy who's funny all the time;
his talk at a dinner party is just as full of punch lines and
needling comments as it is on stage. That's just the way

he is. The guests at the table know it, and they laugh at his barbs.

Why do they laugh at him when they wouldn't laugh at you or me? Because if we did it, they would sense that we're working hard at it. With Don they know he's just doing what comes naturally—*to him.* Without even realizing it, he's following the Arthur Godfrey formula for success—he's just *being himself.*

YOUR OWN STYLE

Another key ingredient in successful talkers is style. They have their own way of talking, and it makes them effective. Four of America's most successful trial lawyers in the second half of the twentieth century come to mind. They provide illustrations of how people's styles of talking differ, but each was successful because that particular style worked for that particular talker.

Edward Bennett Williams spoke softly. He forced you to lean forward to hear him, thus getting more of your attention. That was intentional. It was his method, and it was extremely effective. He was compelling, but never loud. You hung on his every word. And for him that style worked, whether he was in front of a jury in a courtroom or in front of a guest at lunch.

Percy Foreman, another great trial lawyer, liked to play to the heart, appealing to people's emotions in broad strokes. He talked almost in minispeeches. It wouldn't work for a lot of us, but it worked for him. It was *his* style.

William Kunstler is a bombastic lawyer. He's angry. His style is in stark contrast with those employed by Williams and Foreman. It never would have worked for either of them, but it has worked over an entire career for Kunstler.

Louis Nizer's style is to build facts, construct a case. Williams appealed to your sense of the dramatic. Foreman appeals to your emotions and Kunstler to your sense of rage, but Nizer appeals to your sense of logic.

You may not be concerned with how your conversational style would play in a courtroom. But I use these examples to show how, even in very similar situations, everyone can have a distinct style. Find the way of talking you're comfortable with, and develop that.

I've been asked from time to time to describe my own style, which is always more difficult than describing someone else's. I like to think I have some of the ingredients of Cavett's style. I think I could also be described fairly as intense, curious, sometimes aggressive, and sometimes laid-back, with an emphasis on the here and now—the interviewer who, maybe more than the rest, always wants to know *why.*

A FINAL THOUGHT: ON SHUTTING UP

I still remember a punch line my Miami pal Jackie Gleason frequently used with Audrey Meadows when they were Ralph and Alice Kramden in Gleason's classic TV sitcom, *The Honeymooners*. When Alice, sometimes accidentally, sometimes on purpose, would blow Ralph's cover on one of his schemes by saying the wrong thing, he'd look at her with his eyes bulging, shake his finger in her face, and say, "Alice—you're nuthin' but a b-i-i-i-g blabbermouth!"

No matter how brilliant a talker you are, there are times when it's better to remain silent. I know that human compulsion to be part of every conversation—the kids in Bensonhurst didn't call me the Mouthpiece for nothing—but if, underneath that urge, you hear your instinct telling you to stay out of it, pay attention.

5

Trendy Talk and Political Correctness

- Words that inhibit good communication
- How to break bad speech habits
- Political correctness

This is not a book about building your vocabulary or how to speak the King's English. As I've said, I worry about communicating, not about impressing people with my speech. It's more important to ask a good question than to phrase a mellifluous answer. But there are some elements of diction and vocabulary I want to mention, because they *can* affect how well you communicate.

INFLATED WORDS

Mark Twain, who knew as much about talking as he did about the humans who do it, wrote, "The difference between the *almost*-right word and the *right* word is really a large matter—it's the difference between the lightning bug and the lightning."

Remember that the right word—the one instantly recognized and understood by your listener—is most often a *simple* word. For some reason there's a natural human tendency to throw in a new buzzword, or a recently popularized word, to make our speech sound more up-to-date. With the speed and reach of modern communications, new words and usages spread rapidly across the country. Unfortunately some of these new words don't do anything to improve our ability to communicate.

"Impact" and "access" used to be only nouns, but now they are verbs, too, as in "to impact the situation." A plain old word, "affect," would work just as well or better. We also reverse the process, turning verbs into nouns, as in "commute." We used to say, "I commute to work by car." Now we say, "My commute is by car."

We've been using computer jargon, like asking people for their "input," for years. Then people started "interfacing," which was a jargonized way of saying "discussing" or "talking with." And any time we have an earthquake or a devastating storm, we are told of the

damage to the "infrastructure," although the officials using that word would get their point across a whole lot
better if they took the trouble of saying something everybody understands, like "water, sewer, and highway fa-
cilities."

Such computer talk is a reflection of life in the
1990s, but it isn't the only culprit in inhibiting our ability
to talk clearly and effectively. The human ego gets in our
way, too. People seem to think that bigger words make
their subject, and themselves, more important. People today "perceive" things instead of "viewing" or "seeing"
them. Some are not satisfied with saying merely that people or things are equal: they say they are "coequal." If
something is equal, what is coequal?

Others "utilize" things instead of "using" them.
One of the most succinct commentaries I've come across
for encouraging plain talk came from an executive who
told his staff, "Don't utilize utilize. Use use."

I try to avoid pompous language. Some people use it
as an oral status symbol to impress others. Others use it
because they've simply forgotten how to talk in simple,
clear, everyday terms. You will be far better off, because
you'll be better received and better understood, if you
avoid "trendy talk." To say that you're getting input that
will enable you to impact the situation may sound really
"with it" to you, but you'll be more successful if you say
it in English that your listeners—all of them, not just the
computer types—will understand.

TRENDY TALK

In addition to inflated words, our age of instant mass communication spawns a constant flood of fashionable words and catchphrases. This trendy talk is spawned by fads, events, and personalities. Words and phrases born out of trendy talk become instant clichés. Sometimes using one of these catchphrases will help you make a connection with someone you're talking to, but doing it often makes you sound unoriginal, as though you can't think up your own expressions.

Johnny Carson gave us "No way," and his predecessor, Jack Paar, introduced "I kid you not," and millions of Americans wore out both expressions. Howard Cosell inflicted his grammatical error, "telling it like it is" (it should be *as* it is), on us every Monday night during the football season for years, and it became a national cliché during the 1970s. More recently we've heard an earful of "Isn't that special?" from *Saturday Night Live* and "Read my lips" courtesy of George Bush.

Nothing, of course, is worse than using *yesterday's* catchphrases. "Where it's at" was a hip thing to say in the late 1960s to early 1970s. Imagine how far the executive director of a regional organization in Washington got when he told his board of directors that the council "is where it's at." He was another trendy talk victim, because he was so eager to sound like a member of the "in" crowd. All he did was make his directors wonder

why a man with three college degrees would end a sentence with a preposition.

Whether you're at a cocktail party, in your backyard, or on national television, your conversation will
be fresher and more effective if you can minimize the
use of such instant clichés and trendy talk in your conversation.

"NOTHING WORDS"

Certain other words, and some noises, that add nothing
to what we're trying to get across sometimes creep into
our conversation. They merely clutter up what we're saying, meaning that they also clutter up what our listener is
hearing. These "nothing words" are the verbal equiva-
lent of those annoying little Styrofoam peanuts that come
in packing boxes: just so much filler.

Then why do people use these words? Because they
are crutches—oral crutches. They are handy to lean on
when you're stalling, but if you get dependent on them,
your conversation will always limp along.

The unchallenged leader in this category is "you
know." A friend of mine in Washington, D.C., used to
work with a professional consultant who seemed unable
to use three words without two of them being "you
know." My friend's curiosity surfaced at a meeting with
the consultant. Knowing of his addiction, and that's almost what it was, to the phrase, my friend decided to

count the number of times the consultant said "you know" during their meeting.

The meeting lasted twenty minutes. The consultant, by actual count, said "you know" *ninety-one times!* For the mathematically curious, I've figured it out—that's four and a half times a minute. I don't know which is more remarkable—saying "you know" ninety-one times in such a short time or holding a meeting in Washington that lasted only twenty minutes.

It's funny when you think about it that way, but consider the serious side. This consultant, whose livelihood depends on communicating effectively with people, had let this verbal tic become so obtrusive that people were paying more attention to his you-knows than to what he said in between them. How long was it before he started losing work because of his problem?

The popularity of "you know" is being challenged seriously these days by "basically," as in "Well, basically . . ." While you're watching the evening news on television over the next few days, notice how often you hear answers that begin with those words. If you find that they add anything to the speaker's answer, contact the *Guinness Book of World Records*.

"Basically" often appears elsewhere in conversation, usually as a throw-in word that people use for no reason except force of habit. Occasionally its use raises interesting questions, such as the time on the evening news when I heard a police officer explain that the criminal got into the house because the door was left "basically open." Isn't that like being "basically pregnant"? Either that door was open or it wasn't. There's no "basically" about it.

"Hopefully" came on the scene in a big way in the 1970s. Suddenly nobody could say anything about what might happen in the future without saying "hopefully." But in almost every case, people misuse the word. What they really mean to say is "I hope," but that's not what "hopefully" means.

When you say, "Hopefully the meeting will be held Thursday," you're really saying the meeting will be held Thursday in an atmosphere of hope; what you meant to say was, "I hope the meeting will be held Thursday."

"Whatever" is another empty word that usually adds nothing to what you're saying, as in "When you called, I was out shopping or whatever," "I thought it would be nice this weekend if we went to the beach or whatever," and "I have to finish these letters or whatever."

· Whatever you're talking about, try to leave all these nothing words out of your conversation.

Another nothing word, which spread like a fungus in the 1960s and is still with us today, is "like." People made fun of the flower children back then for starting every utterance with "Like, you know," but now you'll hear all sorts of people doing it: "I saw him, like, last Tuesday." It wasn't *like* last Tuesday, it *was* last Tuesday. If you don't want to sound like an extra from *Woodstock,* avoid this usage at all costs.

As if those weren't enough, noises even creep into our talk if we are not careful—two in particular. You recognize them immediately: "uh" and "um." Sprinkle enough of those around your conversation, and people will think you're incapable of talking like the rest of us.

BREAKING BAD SPEECH HABITS

How do you train yourself out of these habits? As with any habit, it takes discipline. Try these three techniques.

First, to use a familiar word, *listen* to yourself. Simply paying attention to the words coming out of your mouth as you speak can be very effective. You'll realize just how many stops, starts, and backtracks you make and how "uh" is clogging up your talk. That in itself can help you clean up your speech.

Second, think ahead to what you're going to say. I know it sounds obvious, but often the reason you're resorting to this filler is that you got into the middle of a sentence and couldn't figure out how you were going to end it. I'm not saying you should script an entire speech in your head before you open your mouth. But you can actually plan out your second sentence in your mind as you're saying the first one, and so on. If that sounds hard, try it: you'll see it really isn't. The brain has a great capacity for letting us do two things at once. With a little practice it will feel natural.

Third, enlist a "speech monitor" to listen to your conversations and zap you when you use a nothing word or a cliché. This can be surprisingly effective. Ask your spouse, a good friend, or perhaps a co-worker to stop you short (they can say "Stop!" or "Zap!") every time you use the word or phrase. Your monitor should be someone who's with you for at least a couple of hours a day. Sound a little annoying? That's the idea. I guarantee that after a few days of this "negative reinforcement," you will find yourself suppressing the target word. By the way, work only on one word or phrase at a time. If you have more than one crutch to get rid of, take them one by one, or you'll be getting zapped so often that your monitor's life might be in danger.

MISSING WORDS

In some cases, *fewer* words, not more, are being used, as with newscasters and sportscasters who have developed a fondness for dropping verbs from their sentences, even when the practice changes the meaning of what they're saying.

When a basketball broadcaster says, "Patrick Ewing fouled on the play," he usually means Ewing *was* fouled. But what he *said* means that Ewing *committed* the foul. Why not say it the conventional way? Reporters and anchors on the evening news often do the same thing, because of the new habit of dropping verbs from what they're telling us.

Perhaps they think it makes what they have to say more exciting, as if the statement were so urgent that they didn't have time to put in the verbs. But it's simply another form of "trendy" talk.

If you still think all these habits are harmless, that one way of saying something is as good as another, try a mental exercise I do occasionally for fun. I find myself thinking about how some of the nation's great oratory would sound if uttered today by the speakers.

Consider these verbless classics:

"Four score and seven years ago our forefathers bringing forth a new nation."—Abraham Lincoln

"I know not what course others might take, but as for me, liberty or death."—Patrick Henry

Or this filler-enhanced inaugural address:

"Basically, ask not what your country can do for you, but what you can, uh, do for your country."—John F. Kennedy

Or Florence King's modernization of *Gone With the Wind:* "Frankly, my dear, it doesn't impact me."

POLITICAL CORRECTNESS

So much has been said about political correctness, and it has stirred up so much hysteria, that I almost hate to use the term. Like it or not, however, we have to deal with both the term and the concept in our daily lives and therefore in our daily talk. It arises from the fact that today, groups such as women and minorities, so long shut out of power in our society, are asserting themselves as never before. And their assertiveness extends to speech.

They argue that *how* we say something is as important as what we say, because words embody ideas and attitudes. I think they've got a point. If you used that old phrase for women, "the weaker sex," you'd be perpetuating an outdated idea of femininity. If you referred to a person as a "Jap," you wouldn't just be using a casual colloquialism—whether you meant to or not, in your listener's mind, you'd be summoning up a World War II–era idea of the Japanese as the "Yellow Peril." These are broadly drawn examples, but they suggest why members of these groups are sensitive to how they're spoken about and why everyone else should be, too.

This fact of life in 1990s America carries both moral

and practical significance for all of us. Morally, to ignore the sensitivities of minority groups in speaking about them is quite simply arrogant and hurtful to them.

Practically, careless talk about such topics can be detrimental to you. Just think of Al Campanis, Jimmy the Greek, and others whose careers came crashing down because they were insensitive in the way they discussed black athletes.

You must be attentive to how preferences in terminology change. I just spoke of *black* athletes. That has been the word preferred by most members of that ethnic group since the 1960s. But it wasn't always that way, and it's still evolving.

When I was growing up and even in my first ten years or so in broadcasting, the proper way to identify a black person was to refer to him or her as a "Negro." With the black power revolution of the 1960s, black leaders said they wanted their people to be called "black" instead of "Negro," so we made that adjustment—in broadcasting and other forms of journalism, in other professions, and in the day-to-day conversation of most Americans.

In the 1980s new terms were introduced. Black leaders said they and the other members of their race should be called "African Americans." Mexican and Spanish leaders expressed a preference to be called "Hispanics," a term now giving way to "Latino." Orientals are now being referred to as "Asians." Many American

Indians said they wanted to be called "Native Americans"; others preferred to be identified by their individual tribes and not by white men's names for the tribes, either.

History tells us that these terms will be replaced in the years ahead by still others. In a recent article, the *Washington Post* listed figures showing its own acceptance of the changing labels. In 1987 the term *African American,* relatively new that year, appeared in the *Post* 42 times. In 1993 it appeared 1,422 times. *Latino* was used in the *Post* 85 times in 1987 and 389 times in 1993. For the term *Native American,* the figures were 112 uses in 1987, 339 in 1993.

All of this proves we have come a long way in treating others with the respect in our talk that we should have been showing all along. The way we talk now reflects the new respect that these groups have struggled for over the past twenty years.

On the other hand, is there a line between respect and paranoia? Do we start to leave reason and fairness behind and approach silliness when we are told that we can't call women "ladies" as a group anymore, on the reasoning that not all women are ladies? One woman (not lady) magazine editor actually made that point to a fellow editor—can we still say *fellow* editor?—in 1994.

You're running a risk when you compliment a woman in your office on her dress. You used to be able to say, "You look terrific in that dress!" or, "That dress does wonders for you." Now you're well advised to limit your compliment to, "That's a nice dress."

Bland, isn't it?

But it's safe. That's the important thing these days: *safe*. When was the last time you had a man (the ones we used to call "boys") tell a woman (the ones we used to call "girls") that she has a nice figure? Or nice legs? *But!* You *can* ask her if she carries a condom in her purse. That's okay to say.

What used to be offensive is now acceptable, and what used to be acceptable is now offensive. As the king of Siam laments in his confusion in *The King and I,* "What was so was so. What was not was not. But now—is a puzzlement!"

Of course, nowadays the king's funny accent might be seen as politically incorrect. But what's wrong with good ethnic humor? What's funnier than a good Jewish joke as long as it's not based on ridicule or bigotry? Or Irish? Or Italian? Or black? Great comics like Myron Cohen, Sam Levenson, and Jackie Gleason might have trouble earning a living today. Richard Pryor released his album, *That Nigger's Crazy,* just in time. Today he couldn't find a record company willing to produce it.

That's the danger of an overemphasis on political correctness.

Let's not become so worried about not offending anybody that we lose the ability to distinguish between respect and paranoia.

6

Business Talk

- Business basics
- The art of selling—and of selling yourself
- Talking to the boss and your subordinates
- Meetings and presentations
- Casey Stengel's technique

I don't know what the exact percentage is, but we can assume that about half of the talking most of us do is in the course of our jobs. I'm primarily a broadcaster rather than a business executive, but I've taken part in enough business meetings as a speaker, panelist, chairman, or participant, and have talked with enough of America's top executives to pick up some pointers that can help you in business talk.

BUSINESS BASICS

It will come as no surprise that every successful businessperson I can think of is an effective talker. In this chapter I'll pass along the tips I've learned from them and from my own experiences, beginning with these three guidelines:

1. The same basic principles apply in business talk as in social conversation. Be direct and open, and be a good listener if you want to be a good talker.

2. If you're talking within your own industry or profession, you can assume the people you're talking to know the technical terms you are using, but you still have to make yourself clear. And if you are talking to people outside your own field, you have to assume just the opposite—that your audience or other meeting participants do not know your technical terms, so you have to speak in lay language.

3. Time is money. Don't waste the time of the people you are talking to. Don't talk about last night's ball game or your last round of golf until the end of your one-on-one lunch and then try to cram the real purpose of the

meeting into a hurried five-minute discussion. And don't try to be the life of the meeting with a twenty-minute monologue when everybody else is anxious to get down to business.

The third point deserves elaboration. Don't you dread getting a phone call from someone you just *know* is good for twenty-five minutes when you're trying to get a contract proposal out the door? And don't you hate it when your boss takes five minutes of beating around the bush before he finally gets to the point of telling you why he came into your office?

Don't put yourself in the same category. Know what you're talking about, and whether it's a chat in a co-worker's office or a full-dress meeting, be prepared. Think ahead of time about the subject, what points you want to drive home, and what questions you can expect and the most convincing way to answer them.

And remember what the *other* person wants and needs to know. For example, here's the kind of situation that crops up for all of us: If you need last month's sales figures, you ask Susan in sales for them. But you don't have to tell her the entire corporate marketing strategy for the next sales year. That's a waste of her time and yours, too.

This doesn't mean you should be closemouthed. One of the most effective ways of maintaining high morale and productivity among your employees is to keep them informed, so there will be times when you give people background information to make them feel involved or to motivate them. But you don't need to give a briefing every time you talk to somebody. You want to avoid that old complaint that if you ask so-and-so what time it is, he tells you how the inside of the watch works.

THE ART OF SELLING

Everybody is selling something. You're selling yourself and your education and experience every day in your job, whether you are actually a salesperson or something else. You may be reading this book because you want to sell yourself better. When it comes to selling, those who are successful in business talk get that way by obeying certain dos and don'ts. You have to learn your products or services—and what works and doesn't work in selling them. The only way you can learn that is by talking to your colleagues and reading everything you can about the experiences of others.

Many successful people have told me this same thing about the secret of successful sales. One who told me is Jack Kent Cooke, one of the richest men in America, who learned this at the tender age of fourteen. Jack's wealth has been estimated at between $600 million and $1 billion, and his holdings range from the Chrysler Building in New York to the Washington Redskins football team.

We were having lunch at Duke Zeibert's restaurant

in Washington when he told me of his first sale. It happened in the bottom of the Depression, when Jack was a kid in Canada and nobody had money to buy anything. It was no time to begin a career in sales. But Jack's mother needed $2.50 to pay the family phone bill, and she didn't have it.

So Jack went out and got himself a job selling encyclopedias from door to door. The books came with a kit telling you how to sell them successfully. With the wisdom and confidence of a fourteen-year-old, Jack ignored the tips, certain he could make sales on the strength of his own charm and persuasiveness.

Well, anyone who knows Jack Kent Cooke knows he has plenty of both, but you need more than that, especially at fourteen. So he struck out, a miserable failure in his first experience at business talk, with a store owner named Mr. Pickering. Then he decided to take a look at those instructions. He sat down and read them thoroughly, taking two hours out of his day to do it.

In his approach to his second prospective customer, he hit the jackpot—because he followed the suggestions in the sales kit. He closed the deal with the clincher question. "Where would you like us to ship the books?"

Then he went back to Mr. Pickering, and the result was exactly the opposite of his first encounter with him. Pickering bought a set of the encyclopedias, too. By the end of the day Jack was able to rush home and give his mother not just the $2.50 for the phone bill, but a whopping $24.50.

"I think that was the proudest moment of my life," Jack says today, "including all our Super Bowls."

He was successful because he followed two rules of sales: Know what you're selling; and once you've closed the deal—don't keep selling. When he asked that question about where to ship the books, he accomplished both—he clinched the deal, and he closed it, too.

There is another key rule in talking to make a sale: Sell the *advantages* of the product, not the *features* of the product. Don't talk about how the toaster has this dandy microchip for consistent "doneness." Talk instead about sitting down to breakfast with a steaming cup of coffee and a golden-brown English muffin. Don't talk about the premiums and payouts of the insurance policy. Talk about the security your client will feel and about the gratitude of his or her spouse and children in knowing that the cornerstone of their financial future is in place.

JOB INTERVIEWS

Selling Yourself

You'll never sell any product that is as important as yourself, so you want to do it right. Selling yourself—in job interviews, in your performance on the job so you can earn a promotion, and in working with outsiders so you can make yourself attractive to other companies and thus increase your career progress and your earning power —is your most basic selling job. Almost everybody in business must go through the process at least several times in his or her career.

Having been through the same experience myself several times, I have my own four cardinal rules to follow. They have helped me, and they can help you, too:

1. Show prospective employers what *you* can do for *them*.
2. Maintain an open attitude.
3. Be prepared.
4. Ask questions.

Now for some elaboration on each point:

What do you bring that's unique? To paraphrase President Kennedy, ask not what your employer can do for you, but what you can do for your employer. Don't tell the person interviewing you what's on your résumé, which they've already read. Tell them instead how you are going to do this job better than anyone else will; make them think about how good the boss who hired you will look. In other words, sell your advantages, not your features. You do that by talking about your knowledge and your skills—the expertise and contacts you have developed in your field and the abilities you have developed over your career.

Openness. There's that word again, the quality that is essential in virtually every kind of social and business talk if you are to be successful. Don't be so businesslike in your demeanor that you stifle your openness. Communicate your enthusiasm for the job. This is a refreshing characteristic that employers don't always find in job interviews, and the applicant who displays it sometimes will find out later it was the one quality that made a difference.

I know a former Washington public affairs director who was told later that one of the features about him that stood out in his interview was, as his new boss told him, "You told us clearly that you wanted the job, you showed a lot of enthusiasm for it, and you told us you had the experience to do it successfully. *You didn't play games with us.*"

A film producer I know placed a classified ad for a secretary. After listing the requirements for clerical skills, the ad said, *"Must care."* Of all the applicants who were interviewed, only one said, "By the way, I care." She got the job.

My own experience in getting my first job in radio in Miami is another case history. I had zero experience in broadcasting. Zilch. But boy, did I have enthusiasm! The general manager of the station picked up on it right away and decided I was worth hiring, that here was a young man he could work with and who was a good prospect. That was thirty-seven years ago, and I'm still working in the profession for which he hired me with no experience.

Preparation. Go over the key points you want to make about yourself. Even jot them down on a yellow pad and review them several times before the interview. And don't duck the hard questions—put them down and then figure out how you are going to answer them. If you've changed jobs three times in the past seven years, expect to be asked why. And if you want to go that extra mile, put yourself through a dress rehearsal by having someone play the role of your prospective employer and "interview" you. That's an extremely effective technique, one that will give you a much better shot at getting that job.

Ask! No one should be surprised to read in this book that I strongly urge you to ask questions, whether you are being interviewed or talking on the subway. Asking questions is how you learn, and in a job interview you definitely want to learn about the company just as much as the company wants to learn about you.

You'll never have a better opportunity to get a feel for your prospective company or boss. Besides, employers respect someone who displays the initiative to ask intelligent questions about the company. That shows you possess two of the most persuasive qualities that we just talked about: you are prepared, and you care.

Harvey Mackay, chairman and chief executive officer of Mackay Envelope Corporation in Minneapolis, has been a guest on my radio and TV shows several times because of his phenomenal success as an author of books about how to succeed in your profession, beginning with *Swim with the Sharks Without Being Eaten Alive*. His third best-seller, published in 1993, was called *Sharkproof: Get the Job You Want, Keep the Job You Love . . . in Today's Frenzied Job Market*.

Sharkproof underscores the importance of asking good questions when you're in a job interview and offers excellent advice about the kinds of questions to ask. As an example, he mentions that every company likes to be asked about its values. "If you can ask a positive question that links the company's values to its performance, you've already gone a long way toward demonstrating that you're with the program."

If the company is one of the industry's leaders, ask about its success. As Harvey says, and I can confirm this from the many speeches I give to corporations, "Successful companies, just like successful people, usually do not count modesty among their greatest virtues; nor are they immune to skillful flattery." On the other hand, if the company is bringing up the rear in the marketplace, you might want to ask, "Which companies in your industry do you feel you'd most like to resemble? And how do you plan to achieve that?"

Harvey also agrees on the importance of *listening*. Once you've asked your questions, he says, "Listen to the answers. Don't make it appear that you're more interested in your own clever questions than you are in hearing and reacting to the responses."

When You're Doing the Hiring

When you're the interviewer instead of the interviewee, you should display some of the same characteristics you are looking for in the job applicant—openness, enthusiasm, caring, and a willingness to ask questions.

Don't just concentrate on qualifications. Draw the

person out. Is the candidate enthusiastic? Will the person care about the job? If you sense that an applicant is shy or intimidated, try breaking the ice with some of the techniques mentioned in chapter 2. If you see something unusual on the résumé—the applicant lived in Hong Kong, say, or worked for a circus—ask about it. This will often get the person talking and allows you to move on smoothly to other job experiences.

Remember that openness and enthusiasm are two-way streets. Be honest about the job and about yourself as a boss. And if you don't show enthusiasm for your company, why would anyone want to work there?

TALKING TO THE BOSS

Okay—you got the job. What about all the talking you are going to do now? It would be nice to say that we talk the same to everyone and in every setting, including the workplace. But it doesn't work that way.

You talk to your boss differently from the way you talk to your peers or your subordinates. That's just human nature—because, by definition, your boss is not your peer.

A second lieutenant in the army is not going to talk to his commanding general the same way he talks to his fellow lieutenants. And he'll talk to the major who is his immediate boss in a way that's friendlier and more informal than the way he'll talk to the general.

It's appropriate to talk to your boss in a deferential

way. All of us are aware of when we're talking to our boss, and our way of talking to him or her is different, in tone and manner if not in words.

But there's no need to talk like an "apple polisher" when speaking to your boss. I don't talk that way to Ted Turner, and I don't know anybody else who does, either. There's no need to be condescending or fawning, and many bosses will hold you in less regard if you do.

In any job, and for many reasons, not just talking, it's helpful to know your boss. Not in a buddy-buddy, "let's have a drink after work" way. But I would get to know my boss for the same good reasons that it's helpful to know yourself in your job setting—your role, your contributions to the company, your strong and weak points, where you should improve, and what your priorities are. Get to know those same things about your boss.

I know this from my own experiences with bosses: if things are going great, you don't have to worry about how to talk to your boss. But if you think something is wrong, something *is* wrong. Once again, listen to your instinct.

So approach the boss in a completely open manner and using two words suggested by Herb Cohen—"Help me." Don't appear fearful or resentful of your boss's dissatisfaction. Instead frame your dilemma like this:

"I have the feeling I could be doing my job more effectively. Can you *help me* understand what areas I should concentrate on?"

Or "I'm not sure I understand how to go about this

project. It would *help me* if you could explain what steps I should be taking first."

If you do, you should be successful, unless your boss is completely paranoid or a jerk. If that's the case, you need to start looking for a new position, not just a new approach. The problem is with the boss rather than you.

TALKING TO YOUR SUBORDINATES

A simple rule of thumb works here: Talk to those who work for *you* the same way you want *your* boss to talk to you.

In large organizations there are often formal employee evaluations, stating goals and objectives for each member of your staff. In a smaller one the process may be handled less formally. But formal or not, such reviews are intended to accomplish exactly what we're talking about here—to guarantee that you talk to each of your employees on a regular schedule and tell them what kind of a job they're doing, where you think they can do better, and what specifically you'd like for them to concentrate on in the following evaluation period.

Personnel management people will tell you that the evaluation meeting to go over these points is also supposed to be a two-way street—that you should be willing to listen to what your employees have to say about *you,* the strong and weak points of the office's operation and your role in it, and what they think you can and should do to make things run even better.

Periodic evaluation meetings with members of your staff are only one method of *communicating* with (not just *talking* to) your employees. But don't just do this every six months. In the day-to-day working atmosphere, tell your employees how they're doing. Give clear instructions. If time is a factor, make sure they understand that, and give them a deadline. Encourage them to ask questions so you can be sure they understand.

Be generous with your praise for good work. If you're unhappy with something, tell them. Don't avoid a confrontation by hoping the problem will dry up and blow away or solve itself, and don't postpone action for a week while your blood pressure goes through the top of your head and you wind up exploding at the employee. This is the stone age way of treating grown-ups, including those who work for you, and it can cause a permanent rupture in your working relationship with that employee and with the rest of your staff, too.

Don't play games with your staff members, either, by expressing your displeasure to another subordinate of yours and "using" them to convey your message for you. Have the professionalism, the integrity, and the guts to do it yourself.

Assistance from Assistants

The employees who used to be called secretaries or even "girl Fridays"—why do I get the feeling I'm dating my-self?—are more often called "assistants" now. But what-

ever title they prefer, such people are the secret weapon
in many offices, the link that makes the whole operation
successful. They save time and get things done more effectively not only for their bosses, but also for their co-
workers, and they can do the same for you.

In my own case, people who work with me know
that Judith Thomas, my personal assistant and one of my
associate producers on the *Larry King Live* staff, is the
first person to talk to about matters involving my schedule. Someone could spend a week trying to get me on the
phone, but in almost every case Judy can field your question herself and work you onto my calendar, a skill at
which she is unsurpassed. She keeps threatening to write
a book about this and give it the title *Call Judy,* because
that's what I tell everybody if we're trying to set up an
appointment or even make a decision over the phone.

If what you need from someone is simple information, talk to that person's assistant first. The assistant can
often pull a file or make an appointment quicker than the
boss. Why leave a message for the boss to call you back
when you are asking questions that the boss can refer to
the assistant? Asking the assistant saves all three of you
some time and gets you the information earlier in your
day.

Show that you respect the assistant's competence
and knowledge. A good assistant is an asset to any organization and deserves to be treated accordingly. Not only
that, it's just being smart. An assistant who feels appre-
ciated and gets talked to in the right, professional way is

going to go out of his or her way to help you—and will move mountains to get things done for you.

How to Talk When Negotiating

In addition to his many other talents, my friend Herb Cohen is a professional negotiator. He travels two hundred days a year, handling negotiations for the largest corporations in America. His book, *You Can Negotiate Anything,* was on the *New York Times* best-seller list for nine months and was a best-seller in Australia for *three years!* He was an adviser on counterterrorism to presidents Carter and Reagan. Herbie knows from negotiating.

One of his first, and greatest, successes came at an early age, when we were ninth-graders at Bensonhurst Junior High, getting ready to move on to Lafayette High. It's a textbook case, so to speak, of how you can turn a potential defeat into a victory in negotiations by making sure you talk from a position of strength, even when the odds are stacked against you.

Three of us—Herb Cohen, Brazzie Abbate, and I—had a classmate, Gil Mermelstein, called "Moppo" because he had such a thick head of red hair that it looked like a mop. When we discovered one day that he and his family quickly moved to Arizona after Moppo developed tuberculosis, we took care of notifying the school. But Herb hatched a scheme where, instead of telling them Moppo had moved, we would tell them Moppo *died,* collect money for flowers, and spend it all on hot dogs and soft drinks at Nathan's, our favorite hangout.

Unfortunately our scheme succeeded too well. After the principal's office called Moppo's home and found his number had indeed been disconnected, the school mourned him enthusiastically, furnishing us with the loot for a massive feast at Nathan's. But it didn't stop there. The principal, Dr. Irving Cohen (no relation to Herb), decided to establish the "Gilbert Mermelstein Memorial Award" for each year's outstanding student and singled us out for praise in honoring Moppo's memory the way we did with our collection.

Unfortunately, Moppo showed up at his own eulogy. As Dr. Cohen was praising Moppo's memory and our good deed at a school assembly, Moppo choose that day and that minute to walk into the back of the auditorium. He was much better, thank you, and registering for the fall semester.

Herbie jumps to his feet, cups his hands to his mouth, and hollers to the back, "Moppo! Go home! You're dead!" Our fellow students, smelling a rat, break up in laughter. Dr. Cohen was not amused. What followed was teenage tension in its blackest moments—but also a triumph in negotiating.

Dr. Cohen orders us to his office and proceeds to do the talking: "The three of you are suspended. You are not graduating. Not this year. Not next year, or any year after that. . . . You have pulled the most despicable act I have ever seen in a school."

As Brazzie and I ponder life in prison with no parole, Herbie takes the offensive. He says to the principal, "Wait a minute, Doc. You're making a big mistake."

"What did you say?"

"You're really going to kill your career if you do this."

Dr. Cohen says, "What do you mean?"

Herb continues, "It's true we're not graduating . . . but how about you?" Then he moves in for the kill: "If you suspend us, there's a hearing. At the hearing . . . one of the questions will be why you took the word of three thirteen-year-old boys who told you someone was dead. Why didn't you check their story?"

Dr. Cohen says, "We did check."

Herbie continues, still brazenly calling him "Doc" instead of "doctor" for his Ph.D. degree. "Shouldn't you have done more than that, Doc? You made one phone call, and the operator said the phone was disconnected. And on the basis of that one phone call, you wrote *Deceased* on his records? We have a bad disciplinary record already, and you make *one phone call?*"

Then Herb made his closing argument: "Doc, we may be suspended, but you're out of work." Then, after pausing for effect, he adds calmly, "Why don't we forget the whole thing?"

Herb's negotiations were successful, resulting in a complete victory for all three of us, his first clients. Dr. Cohen agreed to forget the incident. He also let us graduate.

From that incident Herb began his career in negotiating. Even though he works at the highest corporate
level and even internationally, he can reduce his advice to
a personal, everyday level on the subject of negotiating
something like a bank loan. In *You Can Negotiate Anything* he says:

> Here's the approach to use. If you're a man,
> put on a gray, three-piece bank loan suit. If
> you're a woman, put on a conservative-
> looking dress suit. Wear an expensive gold
> watch and a Phi Beta Kappa key if you can
> borrow one. Have three of your friends—
> your entourage—outfit themselves the same
> way. Walk through the bank, exuding vibra-
> tions that say 'Hi, there! I'm a top executive
> striding through the bank. Keep away from
> me with your lousy money . . . I don't need it.
> I'm on my way to mail a letter.' Do that, and
> the lending officer will follow you out of
> the bank and breathlessly trail you halfway
> home.

Herb's point is that not only in your words, but in
your appearance and body language, you must exude
an air of success, not one of desperation. By acting *as if*
you are negotiating from strength, you can gain the up-
per hand, even when your position is not a strong one.

The Bob Woolf Code

Whatever you might be negotiating for, my advice, based on personal experience, is to talk the language of Bob Woolf. It's no accident that Bob represented some of the greatest names in American entertainment, sports, and the news media. Clients came to him, and adversaries respected him, because he spoke the same way he dealt—with integrity, professionalism, and humor.

That's why I was always proud to tell people, "My agent is Bob Woolf." I always felt that it spoke well of me to be able to say that someone as respected as Bob represented me.

Bob never spoke in threats or with hostility. He considered the party we were negotiating with to be our worthy adversary, but not our mortal enemy. He spoke to them the same way. He never believed in telling the Boston Celtics, "If you don't give Larry Bird what he wants, I'll tell him not to report to training camp." He didn't believe in walking out on a contract or even threatening to. He never told Ted Turner, "If you don't give what we're asking, you'll have to air a rerun on *Larry King Live* tonight because I'll see to it he's not there."

He was perfectly willing, however, to make it clear that we had other options, and on many occasions he did, but he never used the sledgehammer approach, in which you threaten to destroy the other party. That wasn't Bob's nature, and it wasn't his way.

He never believed in costly, short-term victories. He used to remind me that if you make a few more bucks in the short run but you've permanently alienated the other side and this will be the last contract you'll ever get out of them, then your victory is a shallow, short-term one. Herb Cohen has the same philosophy. So does Harvey Mackay.

That's my final advice on how to talk during negotiations, from my own experiences and my frequent conversations with many experts, including these three friends: Keep your fences mended so you can win again the next time. That's one of the many lessons to be learned from these three highly successful negotiators.

If you do what they do, and *talk their talk* as I've been able to describe it to you in this chapter, you'll be successful today—and tomorrow, too.

MEETINGS

Everybody likes to complain about meetings, so somebody needs to stick up for them. There's this much to be said about meetings: When several people have to make decisions or plan how to get something achieved, a good meeting is the best and most efficient way to do it. A bad meeting, as we all know, is torture.

A few simple points about meetings:

When You're a Participant

The best way to save time? Don't go. If your presence is not really necessary, ask to be excused or invent a conflicting engagement.

The less said, the better. Once you're there, if you are not involved in a topic under discussion, avoid the temptation to jump into the conversation just for the sake of being noticed.

Some people feel obliged to join the discussion so others will remember they contributed. It's much better to have a reputation as someone who talks only when it counts than to be known as someone who has to put in his two cents' worth on every subject.

I heard the story in Washington about the time Calvin Coolidge was handed his first paycheck as president. The Treasury Department courier tried to drag out his departure from the Oval Office to see if this man from a small Vermont village had a reaction to a check for that much money.

When Coolidge asked him what he was waiting for, the courier told him he was just curious to see if the president had anything to say about the check.

Coolidge glanced down at the check again, looked up at the courier, and said, "Please return."

His reputation as "Silent Cal" was so well known that one member of a group of women visiting the White

House for tea said to him, "Mr. President, I have a little wager with the other ladies in our group that I can get you to say more than two words."

Coolidge said, "You lose."

She may have lost her bet, but here's another one: You can bet that when Coolidge started to say something, people paid attention.

Don't put other people down. If you go to enough meetings, you'll hear more unnecessary, extraneous, and downright dumb things said than you deserve to be burdened with, but that's part of life. Resist the urge to tell the representative across the conference table from you that what he or she just said is the stupidest thing you ever heard, even if it is. That's a short-term way to make a long-term enemy, and that can't help you.

Be willing to ask "dumb" questions. Meetings have a tendency to develop sort of a bandwagon personality, when one person states a certain premise early in the meeting and everyone else around the table spends the rest of the meeting jumping on the bandwagon. What you need then is someone who is willing to stop the runaway bandwagon by injecting a much needed question like "But isn't the emperor going to get cold standing there naked?"

Don't wing it. If you know ahead of time that you are expected to speak, or if you feel strongly about wanting to say something in particular, make notes beforehand. If you wing it, I can guarantee you'll talk too long and risk losing the support of your colleagues around the table. The reason you'll run long is that you will digress, you'll hem and haw and say "uhhh . . ." too many times, and in general you will make a far less effective presentation.

By all means, don't be afraid to use humor. Meetings cry out for a laugh once in a while, especially if they are dragging on and no one is willing to adjourn the deliberations. I know a man in Washington who suffered through a long, boring meeting on the growing practice of converting rental apartments into condominiums in the early 1980s. After the meeting dragged well beyond the productive point, and seeing that the executive director was unwilling to wield the gavel, this guy says with a straight face, "As a Roman Catholic, I'm opposed to the use of condominiums." Whereupon the meeting broke up.

When You're Running the Meeting

In the real estate business they say the three most important things are "location, location, and location." The three most important things in running a meeting are preparation, preparation, and preparation. So have an agenda, even if it's an informal one consisting of just a few notes in front of you to make sure you cover what you want to in the meeting. This will considerably enhance your chances of meeting your objective by coming out of the meeting with what you want.

Then there are these other helpful hints:

Start on time. Sounds basic, but think of how many meetings you've been to that didn't. Let the small talk get finished in the hallway before and after the meeting. If you allow last night's football game to be the first subject of discussion at the table, you have no momentum for a brisk, decisive, productive meeting. The same applies to letting people drift in for the first ten or fifteen minutes.

Be decisive. You've established what the issues are. The last two questions for each item are: What action is to be taken, and who's going to do it? If you leave this vague, there was no point in having the meeting in the first place.

Be firm. Don't let others waste time or try to score points on each other. You don't have to chide them. Let the clock do it for you. Just say, "Sorry, Pete—we have to move on to the next item." There's no reason for you to be afraid of seeming bossy or brusque. Relax. If you can run a short meeting and get decisions made, you will earn far more gratitude and goodwill than you would be letting everybody ramble, thus presiding over a failed meeting. That doesn't help you in any way.

To avoid bad meetings, remember what Shakespeare could have written about them: "The fault, dear

Brutus, lies not within our meetings. It lies within ourselves."

PRESENTATIONS

Presentations are a form of public speaking, which I'll talk about in a later chapter. But, especially today, many presentations don't stop with talking. In this visual age it helps to augment what you are *saying* with what the audience is *seeing*—through the effective use of graphics such as slides, charts, and view-graphs.

Ross Perot showed the importance and effectiveness of good graphics in his 1992 presidential campaign. He certainly didn't invent this technique. Consultants, advertisers, and people in other fields have been using colorful, easy-to-read graphics for years as an effective instrument in presenting their cases successfully. Teachers know it works. You heard it at school beginning in the first grade—"audiovisual" presentations.

Visual aids have been part of politics since the first flag was designed. Sometimes they even involve a little sleight of hand. One of the most effective visual presentations I know of was described by President Kennedy in his book *The Strategy of Peace*.

It was in the 1840s, and the border between the United States and Canada was the subject of a proposed treaty drafted by the American secretary of state, Daniel Webster, and special British envoy Lord Ashburton.

Kennedy wrote that the way the proposal was presented, in the face of stiff opposition in both countries, led to the passing of the treaty and the harmonious relations between the two nations today:

> The Webster–Ashburton Treaty of 1842 between the United States and Canada was unpopular on both sides of the border. Mr. Webster and Lord Ashburton were denounced for sacrificing the rights of their people. Webster and Ashburton finally convinced the Senate and Parliament respectively, it is said, only after each had used a different map to convince their countrymen and legislators that he had gotten the better deal over the other. The prosperity to both countries flowing from that much-abused settlement for more than a century has been worth several thousand times as much as the value of all the territory that was in dispute.

So when you are delivering a presentation, be careful not only of what you say and how you say it, but also of how you *show* it.

One final note about visual materials: If you're going to use them, practice ahead of time. Whatever advantage the visuals will give you goes out the window if you have to stop in the middle of your talk to fumble around with them or if you're standing in front of a chart or a slide that's upside down.

STENGELESE: THE ART OF OBFUSCATION

Visual aids can be great for clarifying your ideas, but every once in a while you may find yourself in a situation where a little vagueness might be to your advantage.

Politicians, of course, have been doing this since the beginning of time, answering questions with words that don't really say anything when they don't want to be pinned down. The all-time champ at this wasn't a politician, but a baseball personality—Casey Stengel, when he was manager of the New York Yankees.

Casey raised to an art form the technique of saying a lot but not really saying anything when he wanted to duck a question or even confuse the one who was doing the asking. He could be as clear as the next guy when he wanted to be, but when it suited his strategy, he shifted automatically to a convoluted lingo that became known as "Stengelese."

His peak performance, an appearance before a U.S. Senate subcommittee on July 9, 1958, is still a masterpiece. Senator Estes Kefauver of Tennessee was chairman of the Senate Subcommittee on Antitrust and Monopoly. He was conducting hearings on a bill requested by major league baseball to solidify its exemption from antitrust laws, granted by the Supreme Court in the 1920s. Stengel was invited to testify, along with his star player, Mickey Mantle, and the player representatives of several big-league teams.

Senator Kefauver asked Stengel if he supported the

legislation before the subcommittee. Here's part of Casey's answer:

> Well, I would have to say at the present time, I think that baseball has advanced in this respect for the player help. . . . Now I am not a member of the pension plan. You have young men here who are, who represent the ball clubs, they represent the players. And since I am not a member and don't receive pension from a fund which, you think, My goodness, he ought to be declared in that, too, but I would say that is a great thing for the ballplayers. That is one thing I will say for the ballplayers, they have an advanced pension fund. I should think it was gained by radio and television or you could not have enough money to pay anything of that type.

In the thoroughly confused environment that Stengel had thus created, Senator Kefauver said, "Mr. Stengel, I am not sure that I made my question clear."

Stengel, nicknamed "the Ol' Perfessor," answered, "Yes, sir. Well, that's all right. I'm not sure I'm going to *answer* yours perfectly, either."

Kefauver hung in there. "I'm asking you, sir, why is it that baseball wants this bill passed?"

Stengel stuck with his strategy:

I would say I would not know, but I would say

the reason they want it passed is to keep baseball going as the highest-paid ball sport that
has gone into baseball, and from the baseball
angle—I am not going to speak of any other
sport. I am not in here to argue about these
other sports. I am in the baseball business. It
has been run cleaner than any business that
was ever put out in the one hundred years at
the present time. I am not speaking about television or I am not speaking about income that
comes into ballparks. You have to take that
off. I don't know too much about it. I say the
ballplayers have a better advancement at the
present time.

Senator Kefauver, his frustration growing with every word from Stengel and still searching for an answer
to his question, finally turned to Mantle, who was sitting
next to Stengel at the witness table. "Mr. Mantle," he
said, "do you have any observations with reference to the
applicability of the antitrust laws to baseball?"

Mickey leaned toward the microphone on the table
and said, "My views are just about the same as Casey's."

7

My Best and Worst Guests, and Why

- The four things that make a guest great
- Those few who had all four
- Guests I won't ask back
- What you can learn from good and bad guests

Whenever I'm on the speaker circuit, one of the questions I'm most often asked is, "Who are the best and worst guests you've had on your show?" In this chapter I'll give some answers to that question, and the answers have some lessons about what makes good talk.

WHAT MAKES A GOOD GUEST

I measure the potential and the performance of a guest with four criteria. Along with topicality and scheduling considerations, these qualities are a key part of our decision when the producers and I are discussing whether to invite a certain guest to come on our show. If a person has all four, he or she invariably will be a terrific guest. At a minimum those we invite have three of the four characteristics.

Here's what I look for in a potential guest:

1. A passion for his or her work
2. The ability to explain that work clearly and in a way that our viewers will find interesting, something they find themselves wanting to know more about
3. A chip on the shoulder
4. A sense of humor, preferably self-deprecating

Being a good talk show host is a little different from being a good conversationalist, of course. *Larry King Live* isn't about me, so if Bill Clinton came on and asked me questions about myself for an hour, I might have a great time, but I'm not sure my producers would rate it a success. So for the show I want guests who *can* talk about themselves, and especially about what they do, in an engaging way. For the most part, though, I'd say the same ingredients that make good talk show guests would also make good dinner guests or cocktail party guests.

You might not think that having a chip on your shoulder would make you a good conversationalist, but sometimes it really does. If you've just had a battle with city hall or the county courthouse over when the snowplow is finally going to get to your street, you'll be the liveliest guest at the table—as long as you keep your other qualities, like your sense of humor. And if you're steamed because the salesclerk at the department store told you she gets off at five so you'll have to find someone else to help you, that's a chip we've all had on our shoulders—and we'll all check in with our own war stories, and the conversation will go nonstop.

MY BEST GUESTS

I've already mentioned one person who has all four of these qualities: Frank Sinatra. He certainly has a passion for his work, he knows his profession better than anyone else, and he has a certain chip on his shoulder going all the way back to his growing-up years in Hoboken, New Jersey.

He doesn't like the news media and tends not to be forthcoming with reporters, but on a talk show, where he feels more comfortable with the questioner, Sinatra is relaxed and has that openness about himself that is so important. He'll answer any questions about his life, his career, and the music profession, and his answers will contain real substance. Most important, despite his image as a prickly, negative person who might tell the questioner to go to hell, Sinatra has a sense of humor and is perfectly willing to give our viewers a laugh at his own expense.

One story that Sinatra tells on himself is about the time Don Rickles came over to Frank's table at Chasen's restaurant in Hollywood and asked for a favor. Don had just gotten married and had his in-laws with him.

"Would you mind saying hi to them, Frank?"

Sinatra says, "No, of course not. Bring them over."

Then Don goes one better and says it would make him look even bigger to his in-laws if Frank would come over to their table. Sinatra agrees to do that, too.

So he walks all the way across the restaurant to the Rickles table, slaps Don on the back, and says how delighted he is to see his close friend.

Whereupon Rickles says, "Beat it, Frank. This is personal."

Frank delights in telling that story on himself. That self-deprecating sense of humor is one of the four qualities that make him the kind of guest talk show hosts pray for.

Here's my all-star lineup of best guests, all of whom possessed at least three of my four criteria:

Harry Truman—With Truman, to borrow Flip Wilson's old line, what you saw was what you got. He's one of the four-star guests. He always had a passion for his work, he knew current affairs and history inside out, he could express himself in plain, easy-to-understand English, he was plenty feisty—especially toward the press and Republicans—and nobody ever enjoyed a good belly laugh at his own expense more than Harry Truman.

Ted Williams—He was not only the greatest hitter I ever saw, but he is also one of the greatest guests, for all the same reasons that Truman was. He's the John Wayne of baseball.

One of the things that makes Williams a terrific guest is that he hates the news media. People who hate the press often make great guests, since so many viewers share their attitude. Of course, very often the guest who is damning the media has been helped immeasurably throughout his career by the publicity the media has given him.

But Williams never had the media with him in the batter's box. When he became the only player in the last fifty years to hit over .400, the accomplishment was his alone. So when he started ripping the writers whom he once called "the black knights of the keyboard," phones really lit up with callers eager to chime in. When he started talking politics, his views were to the right of many people, including me. But God bless Ted Williams. I love the guy, as a guest and as a person.

Richard Nixon—On my fourth criterion, a sense of humor, Nixon qualified only by a slim margin. He was willing to try to poke fun at himself, but he wasn't very good at it, and his efforts frequently did not come off well.

On the other three, however, he was outstanding. He was a terrific guest, and I always enjoyed having him on my show. He may be the best guest I've ever had when it came to analytical ability. The man seemed capable of analyzing anything and then explaining to the audience. If I owned a network, I would have hired Nixon to analyze our operations and our long-range goals and how we could achieve them. If you asked Nixon in 1993 or early 1994 to explain the threat posed by the government of North Korea, he'd know all the answers and be able to explain them in a clear and interesting manner to our viewing audience.

Nixon had a fifth quality that is a bonus in a guest—he was interested in many different subjects. He could talk about show business, the popular songs—and baseball. Always baseball. Sports was one of his greatest passions. He said in several interviews in later years that if he hadn't chosen a career in politics, he would have liked to be a sportscaster.

He had a team in a baseball rotisserie league with his son-in-law, David Eisenhower. He went to the games from time to time instead of only watching on TV. And when he went, he did two things I respected him for: he sat in the lower deck, not up with the millionaires in the sky suites, and he stayed for the whole nine innings.

That bonus about Nixon—his interest in so many things—made him any talk show host's dream. With

Richard Nixon you never had to worry about running out of things to talk about.

Adlai Stevenson—I interviewed Stevenson on my Miami show in the Kennedy years, when he was our ambassador to the United Nations. At the beginning he asked me to call him "Governor," from his years as chief executive of Illinois, instead of "Mr. Ambassador."

He had a terse speaking voice and blue eyes that danced. He failed in his two bids for the presidency, but running against Eisenhower twice, who wouldn't have? He may have lost, but he ignited the interest of America's youth in public service and caring about the issues of the day even before Kennedy. He was the first candidate I ever voted for, and when he came on my show I did something I've never done before or since. I admitted my great respect for him.

We were in the opening minutes of the show when I said, "Governor, I don't often say things like this on the air, but I voted for you. You're a hero of mine. I have great admiration for you."

Those blue eyes with the laugh lines in the corners twinkled the way they always did when his famous dry wit was about to kick in, and he said, "We've never met, but I can tell immediately that you are a great judge of character."

Stevenson was an exceptional guest because of his profound intelligence and his great skills as a communicator. He could express himself better than anyone of his time—almost too well, which is why he got stuck with the reputation of being an "egghead," an intellectual above the intelligence plane of the average American. Instead of helping him, this quality hurt him.

But it was a marvelous skill to have in a guest. I never sensed any anger in him, no chip on the shoulder, but he possessed my other three criteria in rich quantities. And that self-deprecating sense of humor showed that he had one other quality many great people have: he never took himself completely seriously.

That sounds contradictory. You'd think that anyone who occupies one of the top spots in the country and in the world would be entitled to be full of himself, but the opposite is often true. Many leaders in government, business, entertainment, and other fields have the self-assurance never to take themselves too seriously and not to stay too serious too long at a time about anything. It's another common ingredient among great guests, but not an essential one.

Robert Kennedy—Bobby was another one whose sense of humor helped make him an effective guest, one who was able to score points for his positions by showing the listeners and viewers he wasn't afraid to laugh or to make fun of himself.

The adjective most applied to him in his Washington years was "ruthless." But he was never that way when I interviewed him. This will surprise you, but I rate him as the funniest guest I've ever had. And he had the best smile I ever saw.

Mario Cuomo—Cuomo may be the best speaker in America today, with a prepared text or without one. He challenges you as the interviewer because he makes you think. I was on the floor at the 1984 Democratic convention in San Francisco when Governor Cuomo delivered his famous keynote address. The atmosphere in that convention hall was one of the most electrifying I've ever experienced.

I happened to be standing next to the Oklahoma delegation, and I heard one of the delegates say, "I don't know that man, but he reminded me of why I am a Democrat." That's the kind of effect Cuomo can produce from the lectern on a stage or the guest's chair on a talk show.

Mario told me of his experience as an outfielder in the Pittsburgh Pirates' farm system in the 1950s. He was hit in the head by a pitch and had to sit out a couple of games. A few days later he was shagging flies when Branch Rickey, the talent genius who assembled the lineup for the great Brooklyn teams of my youth, came over to him. By now Rickey was Pittsburgh's general manager. Rickey started talking to Cuomo about his career. "Son," he said, "you're not going to make it to the big leagues. You're not good enough. But you're very intelligent. Go to law school."

In following Rickey's advice, Mario displayed two more characteristics of successful men and women: he knew good advice when he heard it, and he was honest with himself about his talents and about his limitations.

Billy Graham—This man is such a commanding figure that he would be a great guest on any show, and he is always among the top guests on mine. He's unusual in one sense—he doesn't have a chip on his shoulder, either, and he wants to help those who do.

He's a dynamic yet gentle personality, with wide-ranging interests. I had him on *Larry King Live* in April 1994 only a few days after he returned from a trip to North Korea. He brought back with him a message for President Clinton from the president of North Korea, Kim Il-Sung, in the midst of the growing tension between the two countries over North Korea's activities toward becoming a nuclear power, three months before Kim's death.

I asked him if he would tell us what the message was. He said, simply, "No." Fair enough. We moved on to the next subject. Dr. Graham was able, however, to talk about the situation in North Korea in a general way and also about his new programs in spreading his message to the peoples of the world. As always, he was a fascinating and informative guest.

Billy Graham and I make a good host-guest team, and I'm sure one reason for that is that I'm an agnostic.

Not an atheist: an agnostic. (Atheists do not believe in God. Agnostics aren't sure.)

Being an agnostic goes back to my curious, inquiring nature. I've asked many people about God over the years, on the air and off. Agnostics make good interviewers when the guest is a member of the clergy or a theologian because they are curious and keep asking why. Atheists, on the other hand, are not as good in the interview role because they are sure they're right in their belief that there is no God. Agnostics are "I don't know" people. They are curious and keep asking that greatest of all questions: Why?

Billy Graham consistently comes up with good, human answers to that question. By far he is the most believable of all the televangelists. That's why he's been a guest on my radio and television shows so many times.

Michael Milken—"The junk bond king," who went to prison after pleading guilty to six felony counts relating to securities fraud, is nevertheless a great talk show guest, regardless of what your judgment about him might be. He's one of the brightest people I've ever met, as evidenced by his success in putting together some of America's leading corporations—MCI, Turner Broadcasting, Taco Bell, and others.

In my interviews I found him an excellent communicator who gave honest, straightforward answers to my questions. He is now devoting a significant portion of his time, money, energy, and creativeness to help find a cure for prostate cancer, while he fights that disease himself.

Danny Kaye—Danny Kaye was, well, Danny Kaye. We hit it off just great, and not because we're a couple of guys from Brooklyn. You couldn't help loving Danny, and like so many performers whose greatness comes in large measure from their genuineness, Danny Kaye was exactly the same person off stage and off screen as he was on.

Once, when he was a guest on my radio show, a woman called from Toledo and told him, "I never in my life thought I'd talk to you. I don't have a question for you. I just want to tell you a story: My son loved you. He wanted to be like you. He imitated you, and his whole world revolved around you."

Then she delivered the clincher: "He was killed in Korea when he was nineteen years old. He was in the navy during the war over there. The navy sent me a picture among his personal effects, and it was of you—the only picture he had in his footlocker. I framed it along with the last picture I had of him. I've dusted your picture and his every day for thirty years. I thought you'd like to hear that."

Danny was crying in the studio, and so was I. And so was she. Then he said, "Did your son have a favorite song?"

She said, "Yes. 'Dena.' "

Then Danny Kaye sang one of his most famous songs to this Gold Star mother of the Korean War, with no band, no piano, just his voice, through the tears.

It was one of the greatest moments I've ever experienced in broadcasting, because it was such a human one. And Danny made it happen by his openness—not, in this case, a willingness to talk about himself, but a willingness to empathize, and to show emotion himself, that many people would not be ready to share.

Roseanne Arnold—I like Roseanne as a person, and I feel sorry for her. She is a troubled woman. But she's also multifaceted, with interests on many different subjects and experience not only as a successful comedienne, but as an executive who owns and runs two network television shows and other business enterprises.

I enjoy interviewing Roseanne. She certainly knows her subject, she is famous for the passion she brings to her work, she has a good, self-deprecating sense of humor—and she sure has a chip on her shoulder.

The last time she was on *Larry King Live,* she made a fundamental mistake, one that surprised me in an experienced television performer. She wore too much makeup and displayed poor eye contact, looking away from me and away from the camera. I've already talked about the importance of eye contact. It applies at least as much in television as it does in face-to-face conversation. Viewers will laugh about the excess makeup or just ignore it, but poor eye contact, especially in a controversial public figure like Roseanne, gives viewers the impression that the guest is hiding something or avoiding the interviewer or the camera's eye for a reason.

MY WORST GUESTS

Sometimes people you'd expect to be interesting, who have a good story to tell, turn out to be bad or mediocre guests. Again, there are things that can be learned from their examples even if you never plan to sit in a talk show host's seat.

A person who hits the same note over and over again, whether it's political, emotional, or philosophical, makes a poor guest.

Anita Bryant could have been a better guest than she was. My guess is that she was an excellent talker earlier in her career, but by the time she came on my show she was too obsessed with her religious emergence. Obviously that's something that is personally meaningful to her. But "born again" people do not make good guests, because the subject of God and religion seems to be the only thing they want to talk about. You have trouble getting them to think beyond that one topic or getting them to put it in terms other people can understand.

Bob Hope has been a disappointment to me as a guest for a similar reason. In Hope's case his obsession is not with one particular subject, but with one particular style—to answer every question with a gag.

As I've said, he doesn't do this in informal social

settings, but when the camera is on he seems compelled
to perform. He answers your questions in brief sentences
and throws out too many one-liners. He's not abstract or
introspective. I've tried to get him to talk on legitimate
subjects that our viewers would be interested in, but he's
more interested in making jokes. For a comedian, that's
perfectly natural. But the interview has to go beyond
punch lines to be a good one.

William Rusher is a good guest in the sense that he
meets three of my four criteria, but he's a bad guest in
that he drives me crazy. I'm sure he has the same effect on
our viewers, except those from the strident far Right.
He's the former publisher of *The National Review* and a
harsh, dogmatic political columnist.

People from Brooklyn will understand what I'm
talking about when I say that Rusher *grangles* me.
"Grangles" isn't a word, except in Brooklyn. It means
that someone's personality has the same effect on you as
the sound of fingernails across a blackboard.

Rusher's far right political views aren't the reason
he's not a good guest. Plenty of outspoken champions of
the Right make excellent guests. Newt Gingrich is one of
them. So is Pat Buchanan. So is Dan Quayle. They have
many of the same views Rusher has. But they are willing
to laugh, to take a kidding, to listen to a different view
from a caller or another guest.

Rusher is not, and he can be downright mean. When
Richard Nixon died, Phil McCombs of the *Washington
Post* quoted Rusher as saying, "The cruelest thing I ever

said about Nixon is that it isn't any more his fault he was born without principles than it is a thalidomide baby's fault to be born without arms."

Contrast that with someone on Rusher's left, with credentials on political affairs that match his—Frank Mankiewicz, Bobby Kennedy's press secretary. When he spoke of Nixon, Mankiewicz said, "I thought he had lower self-esteem than any other successful American politician. He was the Willy Loman of American politics," referring to the character in *Death of a Salesman* who complained that he was liked, but wasn't *"well liked."*

That's a balanced look at Nixon, one that millions of Americans will agree with. Like most of the advisers to John and Robert Kennedy, Mankiewicz was locked into mortal combat with the Nixon forces and the man himself on many occasions in the 1960s. Electricity filled the air between those two camps, but Frank didn't say he hated Nixon's guts and that the man was a no-good scoundrel. He gave a calm, reasoned assessment of Nixon the man and the president that many Americans from those years will agree with.

Rusher's comment tells you more about Rusher than about Nixon.

But when it comes to my out-and-out worst guest, my answer is always the same—Robert Mitchum.

He was on my TV show one night, and to this day I don't know why he acted the way he did. Mitchum always played the role of the tough, laconic John Wayne type, except that Mitchum sometimes was the bad guy in the black hat. Wayne always wore the white hat. But there were similarities. Both were cast as big he-man characters, short on words but long on deeds. But those were their roles. They weren't really that way in life. Or were they?

I never got to interview Wayne, but Mitchum I talked to. And that's exactly right—*I* talked. I still don't know whether he was putting me on, whether he was in a bad mood, whether he just didn't want to be there that night, whether his dinner was bothering him, or what it was.

But whatever the reason, this guy gave me nothing. As in the following:

"What was it like to be in a movie directed by John Huston?"

"He was all right."

"Well, wasn't there some difference between acting under John *Huston* and acting under John *Smith?*"

"No. Not really."

My next few questions brought answers that were not only one-syllable words, but one-word responses. Everything was "Yes." "No." "Yep."

I asked him about Robert De Niro, one of the most famous actors of the day.

"I don't know him."

I was shocked and disappointed. Disappointed especially for my audience, because Mitchum is so much of a folk hero by now, almost a cult figure. And disappointed for myself. When I was going to the Saturday afternoon matinees at the Benson Theater in Brooklyn with Herbie Cohen and our other pals like Davey Fried and Hoo-Ha and Ben the Worrier, Mitchum was our kind of guy. To have him crawl into a hole and act as if he didn't want to have anything to do with society in general was a real downer for me—not to mention our audience.

The Robert Mitchum episode carries a lesson with it: You can be the greatest interviewer or conversationalist in history, and you can resort to threats, torture, bribery, or anything else, but if someone is determined that they ain't gonna talk, they ain't gonna talk. Don't take it personally, just find another person to talk to. If you're a talk show host, tell your producer not to bother booking that guest again.

8

Bloopers and How to Survive Them

- My own biggest bloopers
- How to set yourself up for a gaffe
- Going on with the show

HAVE TONGUE, WILL GARBLE

Ever since man learned to communicate, man has been making bloopers. In our age of mass communication, bloopers have only gotten bigger and better. They have been a rich part of broadcasting history since Harry Von Zell leaned into a primitive microphone in the pioneering days of radio and introduced a speaker to a "coast-to-coast" audience by saying: "Ladies and gentlemen, the president of the United States—Hoobert Heever."

Of course, bloopers are not confined to the world of

broadcasting. So if you find yourself committing one, don't let it faze you. Shake it off and keep right on going, knowing that you're in good company.

Harry Von Zell shook it off. After that Hoover blooper, which remains the granddaddy of them all, he went on to great success in radio and then moved into television without missing a beat. He is best remembered as the host and actor on TV's popular *George Burns and Gracie Allen Show* in the 1950s.

Just because I can write a book on how to talk doesn't mean I can't blooper with the best of them. If I think back on my career, in among the moments I'm proud of are some I'd like to forget—but can't.

HOW TO "INCULCATE" A BLUNDER

One of the most embarrassing happened when I was doing commercials in Miami for Plager Brothers Bread, whose slogan was "Plager Brothers—For the Best in Bread."

To kick off a new advertising campaign, the sponsor and its ad agency decided I should do the commercials live, on the set during the evening news at three television stations. At the first station, I read the commercial, then delivered the tag line: "Plager Brothers—For the Brest in Bed."

You'd think that was bad enough, and it was. But I did it at the second station, too.

Also the third.

I compounded my original mistake by being so afraid of not doing it again that I *did*. That's one reason you have to shake off a blooper and keep right on going, without worrying about what you just said or did or becoming afraid you might do it again. If you're afraid you will, you will. There is such a thing as what I call *inculcating* something into happening.

George Burns made a habit of this with people, especially his number-one foil, Jack Benny, Burns's old pal from their boyhood days on New York's East Side. Burns could walk into a room without saying or doing anything and Benny would break up in laughter. Burns, of course, knew this and delighted in it. And he wasn't above *inculcating* Jack into committing the very blooper that George used to warn him not to.

Burns told me about the time he and Benny were invited to Sunday dinner at the home of Jeanette MacDonald, the famous singer who teamed up with Nelson Eddy to become America's most popular singing duet in the 1930s and 1940s. Burns set Benny up with this conversation, which was typical of George with anyone he considered a promising foil for his gags, and Benny was always the most promising of them all:

"Jack, are you going to Jeanette MacDonald's for dinner Sunday?"

"Oh, sure. I always get an invitation."

"Well then, you know that after dinner Jeanette always likes to sing a few songs."

"I know. I've been there many times."

Then Burns warns him, "Don't laugh."

"Why would I laugh?"

"Don't laugh."

Sunday comes, and Burns calls Benny to tell him he'll pick him up. Then he adds, "Remember—don't laugh."

As soon as Jeanette MacDonald stands up to sing her first song, Benny collapses into laughter—while Burns sits there with an impish grin on his face. After all, this was the same devil-made-me-do-it character who sat in the first row reading a newspaper when Benny was doing his comedy act in Las Vegas.

I tell these stories here for a reason—to show what can happen when you let worries set up a beachhead in your mind. If you start thinking that a certain thing might happen, you can help make it happen anyhow. You have to *will* that possibility out of your mind. It takes concentration, effort, and determination, but you can do it.

Not all goofs are bloopers in the usual sense of that term, and not all of them are under your control. For one example, we take you to a Miami Dolphins football game.

We're in Buffalo. It's the late 1960s. I'm the color commentator on a broadcast on the Miami Dolphins Radio Network with our play-by-play man, Joe Croghan. Just before the kickoff, a vicious wind- and snowstorm blows through, and I do mean *blows* through, and takes all of our papers with it—commercials, depth charts, statistics, everything. Gone. All the way out of the stadium.

And here's the kickoff. Joe and I knew the Dolphins were the team kicking off because we could recognize their kicker through the blizzard. But we couldn't recognize any of the Bills players, we couldn't see the numbers through the blinding snow, the yard lines were quickly covered with snow, and there we were—unable to see anything through the air or figure out anything on the ground. What to do? We decided to tell our listeners back in warm and balmy Miami exactly what was happening, which is what a play-by-play broadcast is supposed to give you anyhow.

After describing the grim conditions hard on the shores of Lake Erie and just across the Rainbow Bridge from Niagara Falls, we began our broadcast. Our account was, if not classic, at least unique:

"Somebody's running with the ball.... Somebody's dropping back to pass.... Somebody's catching the ball.... Somebody's tackling him.... He's down. No, he's up! ... I can't tell who he is...."

While all this was going on, we still had no depth charts in front of us to help. They're the diagrams showing the players at each position on the field, by name and number, on both offense and defense for each team. Broadcasters rely on them under the best of conditions. Under these circumstances they were essential—but they were, literally, gone with the wind.

Now logic dictates that you do the obvious—call down to your crew for another set of depth charts. But we were on the roof, and they were on the ground. And the elevator was frozen in place.

Joe and I broadcast that way for the entire first quarter. The weather didn't improve, but the elevator did. At the start of the second period it started running again, and we were rescued out of our predicament by a second set of depth charts. We still couldn't see any better, but at least now we could make educated guesses.

The storm wasn't our fault. We were done in by something that was not under our control. But rather than panic and cause bloopers of our own, we leveled with our listeners and let them know the day's biggest "blooper"—the storm itself—was Old Man Winter's fault and not ours.

In another Dolphins game, shortly after Don Shula became coach, their fullback, Larry Csonka, was injured. After the game I went into the locker room for my usual postgame interviews. I spotted Csonka in the medical room, and he waved to me to come on in.

Shula had a strict rule—no interviews in the medical room. But I didn't know this. So Csonka and I are on the air live, when Shula spots us—and my microphone—through a doorway at the opposite end of the room and screams at the top of his voice, "What the —— are you two doing?"

Csonka says, "Who you think he's talking to—you or me?"

Shula threw me out of the room. So I immediately

employed the announcer's emergency tactic: "We return you now to our studios."

At a postgame party later, Don asked me, "Were we on the air then?"

When I told him yes, he expressed his frustration and disappointment that his language had been heard by the Dolphins' fans. I said, "Don't worry, Don—I didn't identify you." But we both knew I didn't have to. Shula already had one of the most recognizable voices in Miami.

A more straightforward howler was the time I was doing the color commentary on a telecast of a Dolphins game. At halftime I told our viewers they were watching "the Baltimore Colts Drug and Bugle Corps."

GO ON WITH THE SHOW

I once asked a guest on my radio show if he had children. The staff collapsed in the control room, since the guest was a Catholic priest. It didn't dawn on me that I had pulled a beaut of a blooper until the priest reminded me that they lead celibate lives and do not marry.

Why did I ask such a stupid question? I'm not sure. It's a natural question in most cases, when you're giving your audience brief background on your guest early in the show. Whatever the reason was, it was so dumb that it was funny. What did I do? Just what you should do—I went right on to the next question.

I was emceeing a large outdoor July Fourth festival in Miami, complete with all kinds of flags and music and a speech by Congressman Claude Pepper. The event was so big that the producers put up two stages, pushed together except for a small space between them. When I was introduced to the crowd, I went running onto the stage, and one leg went right down into that space. I disappeared.

But I had a hand mike, so I made the best of things. I decided to do a play-by-play description—especially since the audience couldn't see me and wondered where I had gone and why. Just as quickly as I plunged out of sight, they heard me over the loudspeakers saying, "I've fallen—don't panic—I'm okay—"

Before long, the crowd was laughing. In fact, it turned out to be a great way to warm them up—just not one I'd want to repeat.

I once *avoided* a blooper—or worse—when Jim Bishop, one of my Miami friends, came on my show. By then Jim had won great respect and popularity as a plain-speaking, down-to-earth columnist and author. He was also a recovering alcoholic who had been sober for twenty-five years.

But—wouldn't you know it?—this night he arrived for my show completely bombed, drunk out of his mind, the only time I ever knew him to fall off the wagon. Maybe he was nervous about coming on the show and had been trying to fortify himself with some strength from a bottle.

When I got a load of Jim's condition, *I* was nervous. Plain-speaking and down-to-earth plus liquor equals trouble on the air. I was afraid of a lot more than bloopers. The FCC canceling our license was one possibility. Also an involuntary trip back to Brooklyn, courtesy of the station, one way.

This was no time to be lenient and put your friend on the air. I had to do something drastic—and fast, to protect all of us. I gave the high sign to the engineer through the glass in the control booth and said into the mike at the table, "Turn the sign on."

The sign came on:

ON THE AIR

Jim saw it, and as he did, I stuck out my right hand and said, "Jim, thanks—what a great hour! You were terrific, as usual." With a slightly puzzled expression, he thanked me in return, then left. We filled the hour with phone calls from listeners.

Z

My costliest blooper wasn't anything I said. It was a sound I made—snoring. Why was I snoring on the air?

I have a good answer to that question: I was asleep.

It's New Year's morning in Miami, the first day of 1959. I was in Miami. I had worked at the dog track the night before as the announcer. Then I'd gone to a New Year's Eve party to ring out 1958 and ring in 1959, even though I never do a whole lot of ringing because I don't drink. Then I worked my shift at radio station WKAT, hosting my own show from six to nine in the morning and then making the nine-thirty station break during *Don McNeill's Breakfast Club* from Chicago.

That live station break was the only thing I had to do from nine until ten, when the host of the next show would relieve me. Throughout my show I kept telling myself, "Stay awake. Stay awake!" I was the only one at the station, but I made it through my show, right into the start of the *Breakfast Club*. By now I had been up for twenty-four hours.

At nine twenty-nine Don McNeill takes his break, saying, "This is the ABC radio network." That's the cue for all the ABC stations around the country to identify themselves. All I have to do is throw the ABC switch off, throw my mike on, lean into it, and say, "This is WKAT—Miami, Miami Beach." Anybody walking down the street could watch me, because the front of our building was all glass. People could look in and see the announcers and engineers at work.

So I turned the ABC switch off and turned my mike on—and fell asleep.

The only sound WKAT's listeners awoke to that New Year's morning was a mysterious drone that nobody could identify—my snoring. The *Breakfast Club* show didn't come back on the air, because the ABC switch was still turned off. The mysterious noise continued, with nothing else. No music. No commercials. No announcer saying anything. Just that noise.

Listeners start calling the station, but they don't get an answer. Passersby look into WKAT's windows and see a man slumped over the microphone. The next development was predictable: fire and rescue units show up, sirens screaming.

They smash the glass front of the building with their axes—while our listeners, now hearing people hollering and what sounds like glass being shattered, continue to wonder. Then the firefighters and medical technicians yell at me, "What's the matter in here?! You okay?!"

I wake up and look around at the emergency atmosphere and all the glass on the floor and stammer, "What . . . ?"

The next morning, the owner, Colonel Frank Katzentine, calls me into his office and fires me. Then he softens a little and says, "I like you. You have a lot of talent. Do you have any explanation? Can you give me any reason to keep you?

I said, "You know what I was doing yesterday, Colonel?"

"No. What?"

"I was testing how quick the Miami Fire and Rescue Department responds to an emergency."

He gave me my job back—but I had to pay for the window.

•   •   •

The best speakers, the best negotiators, the best people in any line of work, all commit mistakes. In baseball they even have a category of statistics for them—errors. So when you commit yours, don't let it fluster you. Remember the old saying "He who never makes a mistake seldom makes anything else."

9

I Gotta Do What? How to Give a Speech

- My "secret" of speaking
- The Boy Scout approach
- Tips on delivery
- How to use humor

Speeches are like anything else in life—there's always a first time. People—even some who are wonderful talkers in a conversational setting—are often terrified over the prospect of giving their first speech. Some are scared about it regardless of how many they give.

We seem to believe that there's some kind of mystique to public speaking—some secret knowledge that makes a person a good speaker. There are so many books on the subject, you'd think you needed a graduate degree before you could stand at a lectern.

I give speeches many times a year to groups of every possible description. My "secret" is simply that I think of public speaking as no different from any other form of talk. It's a way of sharing my thoughts with other people. In one sense it's easier than social conversation because you're in complete control of where the talk is going. At the same time you have to have something to say. You can't fudge it with, "Oh, really? Tell me more." (And saying you have to go to the bathroom doesn't get you out of it.)

This leads to the first key to being a successful public speaker: Talk about something you know about. This sounds obvious, but speakers make the mistake all the time of taking on a subject they're not entirely familiar with, which immediately places them in jeopardy on two counts:

1. Your audience may be bored if they know more about the topic than you do.
2. If you're not at ease in the subject, you may be ill at ease in your demeanor.

So find a subject that you know about, or take a personal approach to a broader subject. If your church group or synagogue asks you to give a talk on your trip to the Holy Land, don't try to make a grand summary of the meaning of the Israeli–PLO peace treaty. Tell about what *you* saw and how the political situation af-

fected people *you* met and talked to. I guarantee you
you'll be more comfortable, and your listeners will find
it more interesting.

MY FIRST SPEECH—AGE THIRTEEN

When I made my first speech at the age of thirteen, I
picked a subject that was very close to me. It was my Bar
Mitzvah, the coming-of-age ceremony for a Jewish boy.
We didn't have much money then. My father had just
died three years before, and my mother was in the process of working hard to get us off welfare, which she
accomplished shortly thereafter.

But she made sure my brother and I had our Bar
Mitzvahs. On those occasions the young man being honored is required to make a speech. I had never stood up in
front of an audience before, except during those recitals
and book reports that every kid gives in school. But this
was a *real* audience—with grown-ups yet.

At thirteen you're not an expert on very many
things, so I decided to talk about one of the things I knew
the most about—my father. Most everybody in the audience had known him, and I shared my memories with
them. I told them I always felt close to my father. He was
willing to spend every minute he could with me, even
though he worked six days a week to operate his bar and
grill, Eddie's.

I recalled my walks and talks with my father down
Howard Avenue to Saratoga Park, where he would buy

me ice cream—"But don't tell your mother. She might think it's too close to dinner." I told my audience that our talks there were more fun and more important to me than the park itself or the ice cream. He'd talk to me about the Yankees with Joe DiMaggio, about going to Lou Gehrig's funeral in 1941. He'd ask me what I learned in Hebrew school that day. And he told me how glad he was to be in America, not in Russia, which he had left when he was twenty years old.

I shared these memories with my audience, and I told them that when I thought of my father, I heard his voice, talking in Saratoga Park.

Selecting memories of my father as the subject of my Bar Mitzvah was the logical choice to me. He deserved to be remembered by me on such an occasion. And from the public speaking standpoint, it was a subject I was comfortable with, knew about, and could talk about with great conviction.

Some of the adults said nice things to me after I finished my speech, and I found I had enjoyed sharing my memories with them. It was one of the experiences that convinced me I wanted to talk for a living.

THE BOY SCOUT APPROACH

The second key to being a good speaker is to follow the motto of the Boy Scouts—Be Prepared. If you're talking about a subject you know well, as I've just advised, preparing the speech itself shouldn't be too difficult.

You will be able to organize your thoughts more easily and more effectively if you bear in mind this simple structure for speeches:

1. Tell 'em what you're going to tell 'em.
2. Tell 'em.
3. Tell 'em what you've told 'em.

If you let the audience know where you're going at the beginning, they will follow you more easily through the body of your speech. At the end, try to summarize your most important points in slightly different words from the ones you used in your opening.

PREPARATION

I'm lucky because I give speeches often enough that I don't have to spend much time in preparation. When I am asked to speak these days, the audience usually wants to know about a subject I'm very familiar with: the new influence of talk shows on politics; Clinton, Bush, Perot, and other presidential candidates I've had on my show; the Gore–Perot debate; the effect of TV and radio on print journalism and what that means for the present and the future; and maybe the Brooklyn Dodgers. So I don't have to do a lot of new homework to get ready to speak.

But unless you're giving a speech on a topic you have already spoken about before, preparation is a must.

You can prepare any number of ways, whichever works best for you.

You can write your speech out, word for word, and read from it in text form. Many speakers do this. If you follow this approach, be sure to practice reading your speech enough so that you can look at your audience frequently and you don't spend the entire speech with your eyes on the paper in front of you.

Others prefer speaking from an outline, typed on standard 8½-by-11-inch typing paper. Still others are most comfortable with notes on file cards. The advantage of using notes is that you tend to speak with more spontaneity, and you don't fall into the trap of staring down at the script. But speaking is like body language and dress—whatever you're most comfortable with is what you should do.

Whether you use a script or notes, you should practice your speech several times to get familiar with the content and become comfortable with its style and pacing. You can read it in front of a mirror or ask a coworker or someone in your family to be the audience for this rehearsal.

It's a good idea to time yourself as you are rehearsing. Your speech may take much more, or much less, time than you think while you're writing it. You should find out how much time you're allotted before you speak and adjust your speech in rehearsal as necessary to fill that time.

SOME CLOSE CALLS

Practicing your speech ahead of time is a good idea. So is remembering your topic, as I found out early in my career, when I was just beginning to give speeches. I've always loved speaking so much that when I started, I went anywhere that would have me. I was so anxious to become a public speaker that I had no requirements at all: Pay me what you want. You don't have any money? I'll speak free. Just tell me when and where. I'll be there.

My phone rang one day at the radio station. It's the chairman of the Miami Shores Rotary Club. He wants me to speak at his club's annual meeting in June. This is January. I say okay, so he gives me the time, date, and location. Then he says, "What's your topic?"

I said, "I don't have a topic. I just talk. I entertain your audience."

This was the last year or so of the Eisenhower presidency. He says, "*This* is Rotary. Even if we were inviting Eisenhower, I would *demand* a topic."

I said, "Call him." End of conversation.

A few days later I'm at the station and ready to do my show. It's one minute to airtime and the phone rings. The producer calls to me, "Larry, an emergency call on line one."

I grab the phone. I hear a rhythmic clickety-clickety-clickety in the background. It's the guy from the Rotary Club. He says, "I'm at the print shop. We're running off the flyer for our annual meeting and I must have the topic of your speech."

This was more than thirty years ago, and to this day I don't know why I said what I did, but I told him emphatically, "My topic is the future of the American merchant marine."

To my astonishment, he said he was thrilled with that subject, that the members of his Rotary Club would love it. So he reminded me: June 10, 8:00 P.M., Miami Shores Country Club.

Six months later I arrive at the appointed place on the appointed date and at the appointed hour, and the parking lot is full. As I'm walking from my car, I see a big sign over the entrance:

TONIGHT! THE FUTURE OF THE AMERICAN MERCHANT MARINE!

I say to myself, Damn! They have *two* speakers! I had no memory at all of ever saying that I would speak on that subject.

The chairman, the guy on the phone, comes rushing out of the country club to greet me with great enthusiasm. "Larry! Everybody is so excited they can't wait. This topic broke our attendance record!" He told me the master of ceremonies was so thrilled that he took the day off from work, went to the library, and researched the subject so he would know something about it in introducing me.

So the emcee introduces me, and he's talking about tonnage and harbor size and shipping and munitions and all the things I don't know or care about. Having given the *history* of the merchant marine, he then introduces me and tells the audience, "And now, to tell us about the *future* of the merchant marine, here is Larry King."

I spoke for half an hour. I figured if you don't know it, leave it alone, so I never mentioned the merchant marine once. When I finished there was no applause, no nothing. I left immediately, got into my car, and started thinking, I'll never be invited to speak again. I'll never be a public speaker. But maybe it's better for me not to. I don't need this.

I'm starting my car, I'm scared and I'm sweating, and at that point the emcee catches up with me and starts banging on the window. I hit the button, and as the window rolls down he sticks his head inside. I felt a great surge of power. With one push on that button, I could have decapitated him.

He screams at me, "We told our members you were going to speak on the future of the merchant marine! I researched the subject and spoke on its history, and *you* never once mentioned the *future* of the merchant marine!"

I said, "They don't have any." Then I left.

I felt slightly guilty. Not overcome, but slightly—a guy in his twenties maybe acting a little on the irresponsible side, but I rationalized to myself that I had given them what they wanted—an entertaining speech. A few days later I found out that the members of the Rotary Club had enjoyed my talk, and the lack of applause was simply because they didn't know what to make of it after being told I was going to speak about the future of the American merchant marine. Still, I could have made it a little easier on myself if I had remembered the topic I'd volunteered to speak about.

I had another experience in Miami that was exactly the opposite. The organization didn't care at all what I would speak about, just that I would be there—or else.

It started with another phone call to the station. One of my co-workers answers the ring, then says, "Larry. Line two for you."

I pick it up and say, "Hello." That was the last word I said.

A voice at the other end says, "King? Boom-Boom Giorno. November 3. War Memorial Auditorium, Fort Lauderdale. A charity dinner. Sergio Franchi is the singer. You're the emcee. Black tie. Eight o'clock. Be there."

Click. He hangs up.

When I arrived several months later, Boom-Boom greeted me with a bright smile and said, "We're very glad you came."

I'm thinking to myself, *You're* glad?

I ran into Sergio backstage and asked him, "Sergio, how'd they get you for this?"

He said, "Some guy named Boom-Boom Giorno called me."

Then Boom-Boom gives me specific instructions: "Okay, kid. Go on stage. Do shtick or whatever you want. Do twenty minutes. Then bring on Sergio. And don't turn up the houselights."

"Why would I turn up the houselights?"

"*Don't* turn up the houselights. There's a lot of competitors in the audience."

"What do you mean—competitors?"

"There are people out there from the olive oil business. Some from the pasta business. FBI agents. Leave the house dark."

So I did my twenty minutes, got some laughs, brought on Sergio, and sat down. At the end of the evening, as I'm heading for my car, Boom-Boom catches up with me, and he's ecstatic. "Hey, kid," he says, "you were great!"

I said, "Thanks, Boom-Boom."

He said it again: "Hey, kid. No kiddin'. You were *really* great!"

So I thanked him again.

Then he says, "Hey, kid. We owe you a favor."

"Nah, I don't need any favors. I was happy to do it."

Then Boom-Boom said five words I'd never heard before and haven't since. It was a question I still remember with a spooky vividness. I remember the position of the moon in the sky over the ocean. I remember the chill in the autumn air and the chill that went down my spine as Boom-Boom asked:

"Got anybody you don't like?"

If somebody should ever say that to you, I *guarantee* you I know what your reaction will be: You'll start thinking of names. I did. But then morality swept over me and I decided not to have anybody rubbed out. He never knew it, but I saved the life of Channel Four's station manager that night.

Instead, I said, "No thanks, Boom-Boom. I can't do that."

So he asked another question: "You like horse racing?"

"Yeah, sure."

"We'll be in touch."

Three weeks later the phone rings again. The voice on the other end says simply, "Apple Tree in the third at Hialeah." Click.

I had eight hundred dollars to my name. I borrowed another five and bet the whole thirteen hundred bucks on Apple Tree, all of it to win. I wasn't going to fool around and bet any of it on the horse to place or show—I was going for broke. While I'm watching the first two races, I'm telling myself, "There are three sure things in life: death, taxes—and Apple Tree is going to win the third race today."

I half expected to see five jockeys "accidentally" fall off their horses just before the finish line, but the race went off without any unusual events. And surprise, surprise, Apple Tree won. He paid $12.80, so I won almost eight thousand dollars. Now Boom-Boom could relax. He didn't owe me any more.

OTHER TIPS

Here are some other key tips, based on my own speaking
experience and what I've noticed in other speakers:

Look at your audience. I've already said how important
it is to make eye contact. First, be sure to look up from
your text or notes. Second, don't talk to the wall in the
back or the window on the side. They're not your audience. Each time you look up from your text, look at a
different part of the audience, so the whole group will
feel they're being addressed.

Know the pacing and inflection you want to use. Some
speakers, if they're reading from a complete text, will
underline the words they want to emphasize. If you're
using an outline or notes, highlight ideas or phrases you
should stress. This accomplishes two things: It guaran-
tees your emphasis will be where you intended, and it
assures you that you won't be speaking in a dull monotone that will put your audience to sleep, especially if
you're talking after a meal.

Stand up straight. I don't mean you have to assume a
parade-ground posture, but stand in a comfortable way,
rather than hunching over the lectern. Hunching con-
stricts your breathing, and it looks bad.

If there's a microphone in front of you, adjust it to the right height, or ask a technician to do it, rather than forcing yourself to stoop like a heron. (If you can, check this out before it's your turn to speak.) Talk normally into the microphone—that's why it's there. If you declaim at high volume into it, you will actually be harder to hear. And be careful to keep your mouth in range of the mike; don't weave around or turn away to answer a question from the side.

HUMOR

Unless you're announcing a cure for cancer or declaring war, it helps to remember that speeches are considered by some to be the curse of mankind. Don't *stay* serious if you don't have to. And even if you're taking on a serious subject, most listeners will welcome a shot of humor.

Never introduce humor with any of these lines:

- "Let me tell you a little joke." (Nobody ever says they're telling a *big* joke.)

- "A funny thing happened to me on my way here today."

- "Here's a good joke. You're going to love it. It's really funny."

- "This reminds me of a little joke. You've probably already heard it, but I'll tell it anyhow."

Why are these to be avoided? Because they are clichés, worn-out ways of introducing a joke or ending one. And you run the risk of disappointing your audience if you guarantee them in advance that the joke will knock 'em dead. You certainly don't tell them ahead of time that they've probably already heard it anyhow. Such introductions to a joke are real turnoffs.

For the same reason, don't *end* your humorous story by saying, "Seriously, though, folks . . ."

What you want to do instead is tailor the joke to your talk. Suppose you're talking to a group of business executives about strategies and how to carry them out. This is one of my favorite stories on that subject:

Will Rogers said he had a plan for ending World War I. He used to say, "As I see it, the problem is caused by all them German submarines, the U-boats, sinking our boats. I propose that we heat the Atlantic Ocean to the boiling point. Then, when the ocean gets too hot for them German subs to stay underwater, they'll have to come to the surface. And when they do, we'll be waiting for 'em and pick 'em off one by one, just like we do during huntin' season back home in Oklahoma."

Then Rogers added, " 'Course, you might ask me how I was going to heat the Atlantic Ocean to 212 degrees Fahrenheit, and my answer is I leave that to the technicians. I'm a policy man myself."

After the laughter dies down, you draw the connection between the story and the point you're making. You tell your audience, "Now that's the difference between *setting* policy and *implementing* it."

If you're talking to a group of engineers, you put a different spin on it. You can say something like "Isn't it great there are planners like that around to make sure engineers have enough challenges?"

The audience responds to this approach for two reasons:

1. It's funny.
2. It makes a point that connects with their own experience.

Here's an example on the subject of problem-solving, a serious concern with many business and professional audiences. You can quote the genius of my friend Jackie Gleason on that subject. He had a proposal for solving the traffic problem in New York City: "Make all the streets one-way north—then let Albany worry about it."

After the laughter, you relate the joke to the point you're making by adding, "Gleason's approach is a good reminder not to make your problem-solving approaches more complicated than necessary."

THE COMMON TOUCH VS. THE LOWEST COMMON DENOMINATOR

I've talked in other chapters about the value of speaking plain English, avoiding trendy talk and jargon. This holds true for speeches, too. If you remember that public speaking is just a modified form of conversation, and talk in your natural style, you know people are going to understand you. They will feel you're talking to them, not talking over their heads.

Don't go too far the other way and try to be too colloquial. Even in the permissive 1990s, four-letter words and other examples of appealing to the lowest common denominator in your audience hurt you a whole lot more than they help you. If you are a marine whose everyday talk is full of expletives, here's where to adjust your normal speech. Even if a given listener doesn't mind if you say "damn," he's going to be uncomfortable if he knows your language is bothering his wife next to him. It's a different matter if you know your audience intimately—say, you're talking to your platoon—but unless that's the case, err on the side of decorum in your speech.

10

Again? *More Notes on Public Speaking*

- How to get the audience on your side
- When to do the unexpected
- The value of brevity
- KISS

KNOW THY AUDIENCE

I don't know how many commandments there are in the bible of public speaking, but knowing your audience has to be one of them. This enables you to establish a rapport with them early on in the speech by showing you understand their point of view.

The trick, in the words of one veteran Washington

speechwriter, is to "hit 'em where they live." Make sure you remember who your audience is, what its interests are, and what it wants to hear from you.

If you don't already know the group, you're going to be speaking to, part of your preparation should be asking questions beforehand. What is your organization? Who are its members? Where are they from? What are the big issues facing you? What would you like to hear about me? How long do you want me to talk? (That one is important!) Will the audience want to ask questions after I finish?

My old Brooklyn friend Sam Levenson did this with great success. He was a frequent guest on *The Ed Sullivan Show* and highly successful in nightclubs, a clean, funny storyteller whose appeal was that he came across as an average person, just like the men and women in his audience. Sam established a relationship with his audience by telling them that he came from an average background, with a father who made it the hard way, and Sam grew up to become a teacher. He made the point visually by the way he looked—short hair, glasses, white shirt, thin bow tie, conservative double-breasted suit buttoned over his midsection.

He'd tell his audience, "My father came to this country when he was a young man because he heard that America was the land of opportunity—that the streets were paved with gold. But when he got here, he learned three things:

1. The streets were not paved with gold.
2. The streets were not paved at all.
3. He was expected to help pave them."

His audiences, working-class folks whose families had emigrated not many generations ago, were immediately on his side.

AND VICE VERSA

And don't assume that the people sitting out there in front know *you,* either. Shirley Povich, the award-winning columnist for the *Washington Post* and the father of TV's Maury Povich, found this out the hard way.

Shirley, an Orthodox Jew and still one of the most prominent celebrities in Washington, was invited to speak at a B'nai B'rith meeting. He began his remarks, a Jew in a room full of nothing but other Jews, by saying, "I'm delighted to be here tonight because, after all, some of my best friends are Jews."

The audience sat in stunned, unresponsive silence, offended that this speaker would be guilty of using that insensitive cliché. Shirley immediately realized the reason: Nobody had told the audience that he was Jewish, too.

He quickly added, "Including all my relatives."

He told his co-workers at the *Post* the next day, "It was a moment of divine inspiration. After that I had them in the palm of my hand."

GOING AGAINST THE GRAIN

Sometimes you can succeed with your audience by telling them what they *don't* expect to hear.

I once gave a speech to a combined audience of prosecutors and police chiefs. I got a call from the late Dick Gerstein, who for years was the district attorney in Miami. He says, "Larry, I have a big problem. We're having two big conventions of law enforcement officials in town simultaneously—the National District Attorneys Association and the International Association of Chiefs of Police. They're both winding up on the same Sunday night, so they've decided to have one big dinner at the Fontainebleau."

I said, "What's your problem?"

He said, "My problem is I have to switch the closing speaker for our convention to that dinner. He's Frank Sullivan, the chairman of the Florida Crime Commission, and he's the world's worst speaker. Can you follow him?"

I protested that nobody had ever heard of me. Dick says, "I need somebody to wake up the audience after Sullivan puts them to sleep. Don't worry. I'll give you a big buildup."

When I get to the dinner, I find Dick wasn't exaggerating. Sullivan drones on and on, in a monotone, of course, and all his slides and charts and graphs don't help. He tranquilizes the whole room, all two thousand people—even puts his own wife to sleep.

I'm sitting at the head table, wearing a tuxedo for

the first time in my life, and looking out at all these police chiefs wearing their uniforms and the DAs, watching all of them nod off. Sullivan speaks for half an hour. When he finishes, the audience immediately gets up to leave.

Dick sees this and panics. He races over to the mike and lectern in the middle of the head table and says quickly, "Before you leave—my good friend, Larry King."

Some buildup.

Now I'm the one who's in a panic. The audience has never heard of me. Two thousand people have just been subjected to the worst speech in the history of the English-speaking world, they're tired, and they want to get the heck out of there.

I go over to the mike and say something I couldn't say today because crime has become such a grave and killing concern. But this was thirty years ago. With great emphasis I said, "Ladies and gentlemen—I'm a broadcaster. And in broadcasting we have a fairness doctrine. It's called the equal time code. It's something I believe in from the bottom of my heart. We have just heard Frank Sullivan speak against crime. In accordance with the fairness doctrine, I am here tonight to speak *in behalf of* crime."

Everybody stops. You could have heard a badge drop. I had their attention immediately. Only now I have to think of what to say next. So I say, "How many people in this room would like to live in Butte, Montana?"

Not one hand went up.

I continued: "Butte, Montana, has the lowest crime rate of any city in the Western World. There were no crimes in Butte, Montana, last year. But nobody wants to go there."

Then I asked two questions and answered them, too: "What are the top five tourist cities in America? New York, Chicago, Los Angeles, Las Vegas, Miami. What are the worst five cities in America for crime? New York, Chicago, Los Angeles, Las Vegas, Miami. The conclusion is clear: Crime is a tourist attraction. People go where crime is."

Sullivan's wife wakes up.

"Another great advantage, when you think about it, is that the money stays local. The federal government isn't involved. The local bookmaker will go to the local restaurant. The cash stays in the community."

I was beginning to believe this stuff myself.

Then I applied the clincher: "And another thing. If we listen to Mr. Sullivan, if we pay attention to his charts and graphs and do what he says, we will wipe out crime in America. Then what happens? Every person in this room is out of work."

The police chief of Louisville, Kentucky, obviously a law enforcement officer with a sense of humor, jumps to his feet, and says, "What can we do to help?"

It wasn't oratory for the ages, but I turned a dead audience around by saying exactly the opposite of what they expected to hear. Once again, a sense of humor helped.

In a more serious manner, I saw Governor Mario

Cuomo turn around a different audience of law enforcement officials with eloquence rather than humor.

I was the master of ceremonies at a luncheon of sheriffs in New York a few years ago and Governor Cuomo was there as the speaker. During the meal, I turned to him and said, "What are you going to talk about today, Mario—so I can tell the audience when I introduce you?"

Cuomo says, "I'm going to speak out in opposition to the death penalty."

I told him, "Good thinking, Mario. A room full of a thousand sheriffs, all of them in *favor* of the death penalty, and you're going to tell them you're against it. You'll be real big with these guys."

Well, the truth of the matter is that he *was* real big with them. When he told that room full of sheriffs he was against the death penalty and then gave them his reasons, he wowed 'em—just through the force of his delivery, the eloquence of his words, and his knowledge of the arguments on both sides of the question.

Cuomo is blessed with uncommon oratorical skills, but any speaker can learn two things from his speech that day.

First is the importance of preparation. Cuomo knew his audience, and he showed them that his position on the death penalty was based on both thought and research into the issue.

Second is the importance of passion. Cuomo could easily have picked a safer, blander topic, as many politicians would. Instead he chose a subject he felt deeply about, and his passion made him a forceful speaker.

THE VALUE OF BREVITY

English teachers tell the story of the man who received a lengthy letter from a friend that ended with an apology. "Please excuse such a long letter," his friend said. "I didn't have time to write a short one." It's not easy to be brief, especially on a topic you know a lot about. But in any kind of communication, it's always worth taking the time to boil down your message to its essentials.

That emphasis on brevity applies even more when you are delivering a speech. The show business expression "Know when to get off" comes into play again. And the best public speakers always know when.

Abraham Lincoln knew it. His Gettysburg Address lasted less than five minutes. He was preceded on that November day in 1863 by one of the most popular orators of the time, Edward Everett, who spoke for *two hours!* We know which speech is remembered today.

Everett knew greatness when he heard it. He later wrote to Lincoln, "I should be glad if I could flatter myself that I came as near to the central idea of the occasion in two hours as you did in two minutes."

Some of the longest speeches ever inflicted on the American public have been the inaugural addresses of our presidents. Such speeches have been known to deaden the audience—in a manner of speaking—but one new president, William Henry Harrison, actually killed himself because he spoke so long. In delivering his inaugural address, Harrison spoke for over an hour in freezing temperatures on March 4, 1841; he caught pneumonia, and he died a month later.

In contrast, one of the shortest inaugural addresses is also one of the best remembered and most often quoted. It was delivered on January 20, 1961, by John F. Kennedy. The new president offered a challenge to Americans as they moved into a new decade following the 1950s, which many considered a lethargic time.

"My fellow Americans," said Kennedy, "ask not what your country can do for you—ask what you can do for your country."

He also spoke of the country's resolve not to be intimidated by foreign powers, at a time when the Cold War was at its most frigid: "Let every nation know, whether it wishes us well or ill, that we shall pay any price—bear any burden—meet any hardship—support any friend—*oppose any foe*—to assure the survival and success of liberty."

Carl Sandburg, the eminent author, poet, and historian who won the Pulitzer Prize for his account of Lincoln's presidency, told friends of his admiration for the Kennedy inaugural address. "This," he said, "is Lincolnesque."

Kennedy spoke for less than fifteen minutes.

Winston Churchill topped that. Early in World War II, he was asked to speak at his alma mater, a re-

spected boys school outside London. Churchill was at
the zenith of his public career, the admired and inspiring
wartime leader for all of Europe as his people endured
Hitler's "London blitz" and for more than two years (until the United States entered the war after Pearl Harbor)
faced overwhelming odds fighting the German army.
This was the advice he gave to the boys of Harrow School
on October 29, 1941: "Never give in—never, never,
never, never—in nothing great or small, large or petty—
never give in except to convictions of honor and good
sense."

Then he sat down. That was his entire speech.

Most of us will never find ourselves in the position
of leader of the free world. Our speeches don't involve
issues of war and peace and the survival of entire nations.
But our speeches are important—to ourselves and to our
audiences. We can learn from these speakers, whose ability to talk effectively was central to their success, as is the
case with so many successful people in every profession.

Brevity is the first thing we can learn from them. If
people like Lincoln, Kennedy, and Churchill are willing
to keep it short to maximize their effectiveness as speakers, we should be smart enough to do the same thing.

KISS

We see from these passages that many great speakers also
adhered to another fundamental rule of good speaking.

It's summarized in the expression "KISS," which means "Keep It Simple, Stupid." There are no fifty-cent words, no convoluted sentences, no technical terms, and no trendy talk in the moving speeches by these three world figures. Follow their example, and even if you are no Churchill, you'll get your message across. That's what makes an effective speaker.

"GET YOGI BERRA"

I close many of my speeches with a recommendation to my audience: "For your next meeting, get Yogi Berra."

That always shocks them. As soon as I say it, I know what they're thinking: Here's this guy who has interviewed presidents and heads of foreign countries. Captains of industry. Star athletes and actors and actresses and entertainers. Brain surgeons. Astronauts. And he's telling us to get *Yogi Berra?*

But there's a reason. Yogi is a wise man. He speaks in parables; on the surface they don't make sense, but out of them come ultimate truths.

Here are some examples of why Yogi makes my list of all-star speakers:

At the beginning and end of his career with the Yankees, Yogi played more than 250 games in the outfield. Yankee Stadium was famous for its shadows, especially in the World Series games of September and October when the days were getting shorter. The shadows gave left fielders problems because they would lose sight of the ball coming off the bat, making for some very difficult catches.

One day after Yogi had played left field for the Yankees late in the season, a reporter asked his opinion of the famous shadows. Yogi answered, "It gets late early out there."

No genius—no *other* genius—could have said it as well. It wasn't complicated or technical—on its face, it wasn't even logical—but it was concise, down-to-earth, and readily understood. In my book, it made Yogi a better communicator than somebody who would have launched into a lengthier and more complicated answer.

When Yogi became the Yankees' manager in 1964, another reporter asked him what it took to make a good team. Yogi said, "Good players." Everybody in baseball will agree with that, and Yogi said it all in two words.

Someone asked him his philosophy of life, and Yogi said, "When you get to a fork in the road—take it."

Another of my favorite Yogi-isms: Someone asked him what time it was, and he said, "You mean now?"

Yogi could make a fortune as a speaker, only he doesn't need it. He'd rather play golf.

11

Cruel and Unusual Punishment—How to Survive on TV and Radio

- Interviewing and being interviewed
- Five tips for TV and radio
- Turning bad news into good press
- Lessons from the Gore–Perot debate

If you become successful at speaking in public, the next thing that might befall you is to find yourself being asked to appear on radio or TV. Don't panic. With the skills you have learned in this book, you are well on the way to success on the airwaves. In this chapter I'll talk about my own approach to conversation on television, some experiences I've had with guests, and some general tips to keep in mind about the electronic media.

MY APPROACH TO ON-AIR CONVERSATION

I think of my nightly CNN show as a conversation that happens to be in front of a camera. I don't think of it as a confrontation. In this I differ from some other interviewers, like Sam Donaldson. I don't feel that you have to come at your guest in an attack mode, or like a prosecuting attorney, to get solid, substantive answers. I prefer to be civil about it, to engage my guest on a personal level, and, in so doing, to conduct an interview that is both informative and interesting viewing.

It isn't going to help either my guest or me if the interview doesn't tell people something, so it must be informative. And it can't be informative if it isn't interesting, because viewers will reach for the remote control switch.

I've already mentioned my interview with Dan Quayle in which he said he would support his daughter if she had an abortion. Careful listening was key in that case, as I said.

But another factor was that I was able to bring it out of him in a way that worked for both of us. Your willingness to keep trying and your discretion in asking your question in a way that is comfortable for the person you're interviewing will combine to give you the ability to draw out an answer.

I had the same experience with Joe DiMaggio Jr. I was doing my Miami radio show on the *Surfside 6* nightclub boat when Joe junior walked in with a friend. My guest was Bill Hartack, the jockey. After interviewing

Bill, Joe junior came on the show and we talked for a half hour about his life as the son and namesake of one of the most famous people in America.

As we talked, we moved logically, almost naturally, into the subject of his relationship with his father. Finally, I asked him the most fundamental question that can be asked of a human being about his parents:

"Do you love your father?"

Joe junior thought for a very long time. "I love what he's done."

"Do you love him?"

Again, silence. Then: "I don't know him."

I'm sure Joe senior has his side of the story about his relationship with his son. If he were to come on my show, I would give him the opportunity to talk about it, but knowing Joe's rigid refusal to talk about his personal life, I'm sure he would decline the invitation.

If my question about his father had been the first one I'd asked Joe DiMaggio Jr., he probably would have given a standard answer like "Of course." But when I came to it after he was comfortable with me, as part of a reasonable and discreet conversation, he gave a more honest, and more poignant, answer.

I have never been afraid to ask what others might consider a dumb question, if it's one I think my viewers will be curious about. I've asked questions with the whole world watching that Rather, Brokaw, and Jennings would never ask. I asked President Bush during the 1992 campaign, "Do you dislike Bill Clinton?" Many professional journalists would argue that the question didn't have a thing to do with the campaign, yet the case could be made that it had everything to do with it because it brought out the human element—one man's attitude toward another—in a person who held the highest office in the land.

We're human beings, even those who become president, and that was a question the human beings watching on TV would ask, so I asked it.

I asked Richard Nixon, "When you drive by the Watergate, do you feel weird?" The last time I interviewed President Reagan, I asked him what it was like to be shot. Maybe a reporter would ask him something else about John Hinckley's attempt on his life on March 30, 1981, but I bet a lot of people wondered just what I did.

Edward Bennett Williams, told me he knew the answer to every question he ever asked in a courtroom, but a courtroom is a very unusual setting, where advocates don't want to be surprised. On my talk show I never knowingly ask a question to which I already know the answer. I want to respond to my guest the same way my audience does, but I can't do that if I already know the answer.

WHEN YOU'RE ON THE HOT SEAT

Your first experience with a broadcast interview is more likely to feature you as the interviewee than as the host. Think of the Boy Scouts again, and be prepared. In any interview the first secret of success is to make sure *you* control the interview, not the other person, whether it's a job interview or for a newspaper story or you are on the air.

You can gain control by making certain you have a thorough knowledge of the subject, then reminding yourself that you know more about it than the person across the desk or microphone from you. If it's a news interview, remember: There is nothing in the United States Constitution that *requires* you to answer every question, or to go into as much detail as your questioner might like, or even to be interviewed. And, as in so many other things, diverting the question with humor when you have been put on the spot will often make your interview successful.

You cannot be forced into answering anybody's questions, including mine, unless you're sitting on the witness chair in a courtroom or giving a deposition in a court case. And even in a judicial proceeding, if you can't remember something, don't let the fact that you're so nervous lead you into giving an answer that won't stand up in later testimony by you or others. If you don't remember, say so. They can never send you to jail for not being able to remember something. If you weren't there, say so. But remember this: If you *were* there and you say you weren't, you are asking for trouble—public humiliation or, worse, legal penalties. Always tell the truth, obviously—and never be afraid to say you don't remember, if that's the truth.

If you're being interviewed in any other setting, including news interviews, don't worry about the questions. If you don't like the question for one legitimate reason or another, you can divert it any number of ways, even on *Larry King Live*. Corporate executives, government officials, celebrities, and even my own colleagues in broadcasting employ some of the following ways of getting out of answering a question:

- "It would be premature for me to answer that question now."

- "I'm not able to answer that question because I haven't seen the report yet."

- "The incident has become the subject of a court case, so I can't comment on it."

- "We have already begun an investigation and will issue a comprehensive report in the very near future."

- "That's a hypothetical question, and I don't deal in hypothetical issues."

One of the worst answers in a news interview now is "No comment." That used to work, although never very well, but it doesn't work at all now. In this litigious society and with the tabloid mentality that seems to be overtaking our society, or at least disturbingly significant portions of it, "No comment" now implies guilt. "If he wasn't guilty, he wouldn't say 'No comment'—he'd answer the question." The only time you hear it anymore is in a badly written TV or movie script.

What if you know in advance that you're walking into an uncomfortable situation but you have to do it anyway? What then?

Answer: Be honest. Example: Tylenol.

When it was learned in the 1980s that someone had tampered with Tylenol's product by lacing its capsules with poison, the manufacturer, Johnson & Johnson, took the straight-up attitude rather than trying to minimize the impact of what it had found or staging a cover-up.

Officials went before the television cameras and apologized to American consumers. Their public relations approach in essence was not to use a public relations approach. They told the truth—this awful thing has happened, but our product remains safe, we have taken extraordinary new precautions to minimize the possibility that it could ever happen again, and you can continue to buy Tylenol without fear.

The result was that public confidence in the product was restored and the company won respect all over the country for its forthrightness.

John Kennedy and Janet Reno did the same thing. When the Bay of Pigs invasion of Cuba in 1961 turned out to be a military fiasco and a national humiliation,

Kennedy took the rap. He didn't say, even though he could have, that he'd inherited the planning that had been started during the last months of the Eisenhower administration or that the intelligence was faulty. He stood there and said he accepted full responsibility.

Attorney General Reno did the same thing after the Branch Davidian tragedy in Waco, Texas, only a few months after she took office. Maybe you disagreed with what happened under Kennedy's and Reno's leaderships, but you can't disagree that they stood up there and faced the music—and won respect for their candor.

Some of the best at bobbing and weaving in interviews are our military officers. The air force adopted a practice long ago of instructing its public information officers that when a plane crashed in peacetime, the local information office was to issue a statement immediately, saying two things:

1. It was "a routine training mission."
2. A board of officers is being appointed to investigate.

Both statements were plausible, and in making them quickly, the air force looked positive and responsible to the public's right to know about the accident. At the same time, saying these two things blunted any charges or suspicions and brought the air force valuable time while it went on with the business of launching an investigation.

OTHER WEAPONS AT YOUR DISPOSAL

Here are five tips, picked up from my own experiences and from talking to others in broadcasting, that will help you to survive and succeed on radio and TV:

1. Do only what makes you comfortable.
2. Stay current.
3. Don't think negative.
4. Approach both radio and TV essentially the same way.
5. Work to improve those elements that are important—voice, delivery, appearance if it's TV.

Stick with what makes you comfortable—One of the secrets for a successful performance in representing yourself, your company, or your organization on radio or television is to make sure you're comfortable with what you're doing. If you don't want to be interviewed, don't do it. If somebody shoves a mike in your face on your way out of a meeting, employ one of the responses I've suggested. Follow the advice Jackie Gleason used to give: "I want to enjoy what I'm doing. I don't want to feel as if I'm working."

If it's a subject you're not comfortable with or you don't feel you know enough about, decline the interview. Send someone else. Or just tell them they got the wrong guy.

Stay current—Remain "young" in the sense that you stay current. Know what TV shows and movies are popular, who the favorite singers and actors are. Have a working familiarity, not necessarily an expert's knowledge, on the stories of the day and what news people are talking about.

When I was in my teens, twenties, and thirties, the celebrities were people like Frank Sinatra, Glenn Miller, Joe DiMaggio, and Franklin Roosevelt. But as I grew older the names changed, and so did the times. Soon we were talking about Jackie Robinson and Dwight Eisenhower, then JFK and Elvis. Today we have to know who Tom Cruise and Roseanne Arnold are. Instead of the jitterbugging and bobby-soxers of my youth, I have to know something about rock and even rap music. I may not like it, but I have to know there is such a thing.

In the 1950s and later, we had to know a little something about the Cold War. Now we have to know about its end. We used to need to be conversant about the Soviet Union. Now we also have to be able to talk to some extent about Bosnia.

That's one of the major reasons President Clinton has appeared on MTV. Clinton agrees to go on that show not just to *stay* current, but to *show* he's current, that he knows the interests and concerns of America's youth and their parents who vote.

Avoid negatives—Don't worry about negatives, that you might not do well. If you concentrate on negatives, your performance will be negative. Remind yourself that your appearance on the show or your answers in the interview, although they may be important to you and maybe to many others, will probably not change the course of civilization as we know it.

John Lowenstein, a talented major-league baseball player for sixteen years and now a broadcaster on the Baltimore Orioles' telecasts, was once asked by a reporter about his failure to lay down a bunt at a decisive point in that night's Orioles game.

Lowenstein, maybe the most original philosopher in baseball since Casey Stengel and Yogi Berra, told the reporter, "Look—there are a billion people living in China, and tomorrow morning not one of them will know I missed that bunt."

So relax.

Approach radio and TV the same way—On television your appearance is important. On radio it isn't. Beyond that, I approach both the same way.

I'm a communicator—a verbal communicator. During my thirty-seven years on radio, I looked at my guests the same way I look at them on television. On TV I let the camera follow me; I don't follow it. Because appearance is not important on radio, I often wore jeans; I never do on TV. Sometimes I have lunch in white shirt and tie (although I may wear my 1937 Dodgers warm-up jacket instead of a suit or sport coat), go home to my condo in Arlington, Virginia, and change into jeans, then change into dress shirt, tie, and suspenders for my night-time TV show.

Improve your voice and look your best—On both radio and television, your voice is important. Maybe it shouldn't be, but it is. Your speaking voice projects distinction and authority. Some have made it big in broadcasting without a great voice. Edwin Newman is one example. So was Red Barber. But they are exceptions. They have overcome their lack of a great voice by projecting distinction and authority in other ways—with a talented delivery, interpretive skills in knowing how to talk about their subject, and a thorough knowledge of and deep passion for their topic.

I'm lucky to have been born with what is considered a good voice for broadcasting. I've never had to worry about it. But if I didn't have the voice I've been given, I would seek to improve it, even if I never went on the air for anything. It is too much of a factor in your success. It has been said that President Clinton would project a more persuasive image if he had a stronger and deeper voice, although I don't know how anyone could be more impressive on television than he is. He's our best TV president since Kennedy, including Reagan. But if you can imagine Clinton with Edward R. Murrow's voice, you'll see what I mean.

In any profession, if I thought my voice could stand improving, I would find a voice teacher—they're in every city—or read books in the library or do both. I know from others in broadcasting that voice training works, and so do voice exercises. If your voice is an important part of your job, and you can *make* it important and beneficial to you, I would ask myself if it could be better. If so, you can take the suggestions above. Then apply the punch line to that old joke about the young violinist who asked an elderly one on the street how to get to Carnegie Hall—"practice, practice, practice."

No matter what the quality of your voice is, your delivery is very important. If you sound too much like Don Knotts or if people tell you that you don't talk loud enough or you talk too fast, work on it. Slow yourself down; this will in turn *calm* you down. The best way to do that is to get used to the sound of your own voice, and that's another key ingredient in determining your success or failure on radio or TV.

The first time you heard yourself on a tape recording, even if it was the message on your telephone answering machine, I know exactly what you said: "Oh! I sound awful!"

The truth of the matter is that everyone thinks and says the same thing the first time they hear their own voice. So if you're going to be on radio or television, you should make sure you are comfortable with the sound of your voice. How? By talking out loud, the same way many speakers do in rehearsing a speech.

Practice answering imaginary questions, or have someone conduct a "dry run" with you, the same way experienced leaders in business and government do before they appear on a broadcast or at a press conference. Get used to what you sound like, and develop your own pace in speaking, one that comes naturally to you and helps to make you comfortable. You'll feel much calmer and more assured when you go on the air, and this will greatly enhance your chances for a successful, persuasive performance.

When you're on television, your appearance becomes extremely important because you are representing not only someone else, but yourself, too. So you want to wear a good-looking suit or dress and make sure you're well groomed, even down to such basics as clean fingernails. We don't need to go into a discussion of personal hygiene here, but—trust me on this—that television camera doesn't lie. It shows the viewer *exactly* what you look like. If the third button on your shirt or blouse is unbuttoned, the viewers will see it. If your fingernails have black edges because you changed the oil in your car that afternoon, the viewers will see that, too.

On the positive side, if your hair looks great and so does the rest of you, you will represent yourself and your organization effectively, especially on TV.

DEALING WITH THE MEDIA: A TEXTBOOK CASE

Here's an example of how one organization that had suffered a serious setback dealt with the media in a forthright manner and not only salvaged but improved its reputation.

In Montgomery County, Maryland, just outside Washington, three prisoners staged an overnight jail break in the 1960s. The next morning the county's information officer called all the papers and radio and TV stations in Washington and the Maryland suburbs and invited them to a press conference and a tour of the jail, telling the reporters and editors that county officials were going to lay open everything. They were going to show reporters and photographers what happened, how it happened, and the part of the county jail where the prisoners made their escape.

While they were on their way to the county seat in Rockville, the information officer met with the county manager, Mason Butcher, a respected, positive-thinking, and capable executive, to advise him on what to say to the media.

When the media arrived, Butcher and the warden were there to answer questions. And that's exactly what they did—*answer* questions, instead of saying "No comment" or displaying an evasive or even hostile attitude toward the media. Then—all of this is true—Butcher and his staff actually escorted the media on a guided tour of the jail, showing them the spot of the breakout and the materials and equipment used when the prisoners made their break for freedom.

Acting on the earlier advice of his information of-

ficer—an air force veteran with a good memory—
Butcher then announced that a board of officials was
being appointed to investigate the break and make recommendations on how to prevent escapes in the future.

The escapees were rounded up in short order. A few
months later the special commission issued its reports
and made its recommendations. Not long after that, the
warden retired.

What could have been a humiliating experience for
the county government and a disaster for everybody except the prisoners turned out to be a public relations triumph. The local newspaper published an editorial of
praise, citing the officials for their enlightened attitude in
handling the situation.

The interviewees could have done just the opposite
and suffered far worse consequences. Instead, they chose
the up-front attitude—and came out with a big win for
themselves. Besides being a textbook case in media relations, in which the officials turned a negative into a positive, it was a classic case of how to handle questions
from the media with an attitude and performance that
benefits all parties concerned, especially you.

HUMOR AND HUMORLESSNESS

President Kennedy was a master in the use of humor to
deflect a question. During his presidency, the Young
Democrats expressed their dissatisfaction with some of

his policies. When a reporter asked him about this at a televised press conference, JFK did not go into any long, belabored defense of his policies.

Instead he smiled and said, "I don't know what's wrong with the Young Democrats and the Young Republicans—but, fortunately, time is on our side." Instead of putting himself on the defensive, he made fun of their tender ages, got a laugh, and won the round.

President Nixon had trouble doing this. During the depths of his Watergate days, Dan Rather asked Nixon a question at a nationally televised prime-time news conference, one that clearly aggravated Nixon. Instead of answering it forthrightly or kissing it off and going on to the next question, Nixon shot back, "Are you running for something?"

Whereupon Rather responded, "No, sir. Are you?"

Some viewers criticized Rather as being disrespectful, but others thought a legitimate question deserved a legitimate answer instead of a presidential insult. And everyone agreed that Nixon, unlike Kennedy ten years earlier, lost the round.

Below the presidential level, a politician in Fairfax County, Virginia, who headed a special committee, paid a certain price a few years ago for not being on top of his subject.

When an elected official from another county asked him—in front of reporters, microphones, and cameras—about a sensitive part of his committee's work, one that

the chairman was clearly not prepared to deal with, he
sputtered his response, sprinkled liberally with uhs after
every second or third word: "It is the position of the committee that the committee is not in a position to take a
position at this time."

THE GORE–PEROT DEBATE

When Vice President Gore and Ross Perot appeared on
Larry King Live to debate the North American Free
Trade Agreement in 1993, they performed what turned
out to be a textbook case on how to talk, how to use
body language, and how to accidentally defeat yourself
by making fundamental mistakes.

It started with a phone call to my apartment at
eight-thirty on a Thursday morning in the fall of 1993.

The caller said, "Larry? Al."

I said, "Al who?"

"Al Gore." The discussion got better after that.

The vice president said he wanted to debate Ross
Perot on NAFTA. The agreement was about to be voted
on in Congress, and it looked as though the administration, which was pushing NAFTA, would lose. Critics of
the agreement, among them Ross Perot, seemed to have a
majority on their side. Even getting the green light from
President Clinton to make the pitch to us was a victory
for Gore, because he and Clinton were the only two members of their own administration who wanted to take on

Perot. Everyone else argued that Perot would eat Gore alive, that they would be giving Perot a lot of national exposure to pick up even more votes, that they would be giving Perot the kind of platform—national television— where he had always performed so persuasively.

Perot underestimated his opponent. In addition to Gore's superior knowledge of the subject, his conduct was exemplary, the result of his experience in the Senate, where you never lose your cool, never display your disrespect for your opponent, look him squarely in the eye, remain firm in your responses, and refrain from ridiculing your worthy adversary. In contrast, Perot was short-tempered, resorted to sound bites while decrying that practice, used poor body language, and prompted some viewers to wonder whether, as a billionaire business executive, he was unaccustomed to being challenged.

Body language, intentional or natural, had a great deal to do with what was widely considered to be a victory by Gore and a defeat for Perot. Gore sat at an angle so he could look Perot in the eye. Perot sat facing me and avoided Gore's eyes as much as possible. Gore looked relaxed and confident. Perot looked combative and irritated. Gore spoke with assurance. Perot kept complaining that Gore wouldn't let him finish. To many of our viewers he came across as a classic example of someone with insufficient experience and knowledge on the subject, trying to debate someone who was thoroughly familiar with it, primed and ready for debate.

One of the refreshing qualities about Ross Perot is his positive nature. He still doesn't believe he lost that debate. And he's still friendly toward Gore and me. I ran into Perot four days later, and by then I hadn't heard anything else for four days except what a blockbuster show it was and how we had written political and television history that night. So I said to him, "Ross, when I die, your name is going to be in the first paragraph of my obituary."

He said, "And yours will be in mine."

I knew I had a "first" going in. And the results showed it. That program produced the largest audience in the history of cable television—twenty-five million viewers. And now anything is possible. You will see presidents, not just vice presidents, willing and even anxious to debate private citizens on other private issues.

Television is changing not only the way we live, but the way we govern, and the Gore–Perot debate was a dramatic demonstration of how TV will influence our lives. It was a dazzling look into the way things will be done in the future, how we will conduct the business of government.

President Clinton commented on that in a letter to me when the American Friends of Hebrew University selected me as the 1994 winner of their Scopus Award. In a light vein, Clinton wondered how our Founding Fathers might have written at least one part of the Constitution differently if they were writing it today.

"The Constitution requires periodic reports to the

Congress by the president of the state of the Union. What were they thinking? If they knew then what we know now, they would know that with a few guests and opening up the phone lines, you can assess the state of the Union and, indeed, the state of the world every day, live and on CNN."

It was an exaggeration—but maybe not for long.

Before the Gore–Perot debate, I reminded myself of something I am aware of in all such settings, something that baseball umpires and officials in all other sports should never forget: Nobody comes to watch the umpire perform. When Gore and Perot debated NAFTA on my show, I knew beforehand that nobody was going to tune in to watch *me* and see how I performed. Gore and Perot were the attraction, so I maintained a low profile.

My role that night was similar to one you might find yourself in from time to time in your career, so maybe my view of the role can help you the next time you are the moderator of a panel discussion, a roundtable session, or any other kind of event at a meeting, seminar, or workshop.

It applies to any setting involving two or more persons who are discussing or debating the pros and cons of a proposal or issue. If you are the moderator, remain impartial, keep the discussion moving, make sure both sides get equal time, keep the participants on the subject, and control the tone, length, and content of questions from the audience. A congressional bill may not be hanging in the balance, but it will probably be part of something that is important to you. If you're a good umpire, you'll have done your job, and the participants will walk away friends.

12

Future Talk

THE FUTURE IS NOT WHAT IT USED TO BE

I chaired a panel session in New Orleans in May 1994 on one of the subjects we hear about so often in the 1990s—the "information superhighway." It was a fascinating occasion, sponsored by Newbridge Networks Inc. of Herndon, Virginia, just outside Washington. As speakers Newbridge attracted executives of some of the leading companies in this field.

Their discussion left me with one unshakable thought as my plane headed back to Washington: The future is not what it used to be.

That's not meant to be a cute line or a clever play on words. It's the only conclusion you could come to if you had sat on that stage next to me and listened to those executives who are experts in the way we communicate now, the way we'll be doing it in the future, and the fundamental changes being brought about in our lives.

As these experts pointed out, the "information superhighway" is already here. What we're doing now is adding more lanes. We already have pagers, fax machines, cellular telephones, videocassette recorders, answering machines and voice mail, palmtop computers, and electronic bulletin boards. The next ten years will bring even more communications devices.

IS TALK OBSOLETE?

Some people are afraid that with so much information being carried in so many electronic media, the art of conversation will become obsolete. I'd say exactly the opposite. We're "talking" more than ever, and in more *ways* than ever, because of all these new devices. But conversation will be with us as long as there are humans. In fact, at this conference I was struck by the thought that whatever new technologies the twenty-first century brings us, the first few words of this book will still hold true: "We've all gotta talk."

And with all the inventions and Star Wars developments before us, success will always come back to basics. Whether you're sitting across a table from somebody or typing messages across a computer network, the principles of good talk are the same. It's all about making a connection with the other person.

Openness, enthusiasm, and a willingness to listen will make you a popular conversationalist in any medium. And whether you're talking to twelve people in a community center or giving a satellite teleconference, it's the same with addressing a group. Preparation, knowing your audience, and keeping it simple will always make you a successful speaker.

A FINAL WORD

As I finish writing this book, I'm even more convinced than when I started that there's always more you can learn about the art of talking, and that this book can help you. How do I know? Because it has already helped me. Writing it has reminded me of some of the ideas and techniques that we tend to get away from occasionally as we hurry through our busy lives.

In Chapter 10 I mentioned Shirley Povich of the *Washington Post*. He became one of America's most respected journalists by following his personal creed: "The story has never been written that couldn't have been written better."

That goes for talking, too. No matter how much we know about it, we can continue to improve the way we talk and achieve the success and confidence that comes with that improvement. Even somebody who has been at it as long as I have, and for a living no less, can—and should—keep practicing these techniques. Herb Cohen may be less than thrilled to hear that I want more practice talking, because he's already been listening to me for five decades. But he can be thankful for one thing: I don't give the complete account any more of the baseball games I go to. They last more than three hours now.

If there's one thing I hope you get out of this book, it's an attitude about talk. Talk should not be a challenge, a grim obligation, or a way of filling up time. Talk is mankind's greatest invention, it's how we make connections among us, and it's one of the pleasures that life has to offer. Think of every conversation as an opportunity.

Regardless of your ability as a talker, remember this:

1. If you feel you're not good at it, you can be.
2. If you feel you *are* good at it, you can be better.

Keep talking!